EMPOWER YOUR PURPOSE

Empower Your Purpose

7 Keys to Achieve Success and Fulfill Your Destiny

JARED SAWYER JR.

JSJ ENTERPRISES
Atlanta

EMPOWER YOUR PURPOSE
Copyright © 2017 by Jared Sawyer Jr. All rights reserved.

No part of this publication may be reproduced, stored in a retrieval system or transmitted in any way by any means, electronic, mechanical, photocopy, recording or otherwise without the prior permission of the author except as provided by USA copyright law.

This book is designed to provide accurate and authoritative information with regard to the subject matter covered. This information is given with the understanding that neither the author nor JSJ Enterprises LLC is engaged in rendering legal, professional advice. Since the details of your situation are fact dependent, you should additionally seek the services of a competent professional.

The opinions expressed by the author are not necessary those of JSJ Enterprises LLC.

Published by JSJ Enterprises LLC
www.itsjsjent.com

Book design & photography by Monroe Media

Published in the United States of America

ISBN-13: 978-0-692-98517-5
Religion / Christian Life / Inspirational

Also from Jared Sawyer Jr.

WALKING IN VICTORY: 4 Power Tips to Help You Reach Your Potential In God
9-1-1: The Spiritual Emergency System
I BELONG TO GOD: Staying On The Christian Path To Success

CONTENTS

Acknowledgements
Preface
Introduction

KEY #1 - DO AND DARE

Go After Your Vision
Double Your Failure Rate
Stretch Your Capacity
Build Self-Confidence Through Taking Action

KEY #2 - BE CONSISTENT

Increase Your Productivity
Becoming more Effective and Efficient
Valuing Your Time

KEY #3 - BE TRANSPARENT

Mentorship Matters
Your Network is Your Net Worth
Clear Communication Requires Clear Thinking
Make People Feel Important & Empower Others
Valuing Relationships: Leads to Customers
Keep It Simple

KEY #4 - BE HUMBLE

Accept Feedback and Assume Responsibility
Curiosity & "Thank You" goes a long way

KEY #5 - COMMIT TO EXCELLENCE

Exceptionality at its Best
Innovation vs. Imagination
Learn from your mistakes
Stop being nice to yourself

KEY #6 – CENTER YOUR BALANCE

Start with a dream
Protect yourself from burnout
Plan, Plan, Plan

KEY #7 – KEEP YOUR FOCUS

Define your brand
Be a leader, not a boss

Acknowledgements

Any good book comes into existence through an author's meticulous labor and the support of many people. This is my fourth and each writing experience is taken up as a duteous and pedantic task.

Gathering raw thoughts and ideas, filtering it through an extensive refining process and shaping them into a finely tuned piece of literature for people to enjoy and embrace takes a great team of people who are proficient and just as enthusiastic, if not more, than you. They become a vital piece in seeing your dream become reality. I've been blessed to have just such a team working with me on this book and I genuinely value each person who has contributed.

First, I want to thank the people who have poured into my spirit, starting with my pastor, Reverend Dr. William E. Flippin Sr. and the Greater Piney Grove Baptist Church family.

To all in the body of Christ who I have been graced to encounter over the past 15 years in ministry traveling the world – it has been a divine privilege to meet and talk with a wide variety of men and women of God who are motivated by what God has done, continues to do, and has in store of his people. Your constant affirmation that our best days are still ahead of us have inspired me to move forward with hope and confidence.

Next, I want to thank the many great authors whose books have helped shape my life, as well, to include Bishop T.D. Jakes, Dr. Bill Winston, and the late Dr. Myles Munroe. Those mentors contributed greatly to my continual writing and speaking.

I am grateful to my mother and father for laying the strong foundations on which much of what I do today is built. My maternal grandparents, Lonnie & Miriam Almond, and paternal grandparents, Sherryln & James Sawyer – you all have been instrumental in the development of my spiritual acumen.

To Tricia Harris – thank you for being a mentor and helping to see to it the writing of this very book and its success. To my executive assistant, Jenna Sims – you have been a central force in my ministry and businesses and am so grateful for you.

I want to extend a heartfelt thanks to my mom, Sabrina Sawyer, who loves me, prays for me, and always encourages me to reach my God-given potential and my sister, Emani, who is a genuine beacon of light.

With every life that is touched through my books, speaking, video ministries, social media, you share the credit.

Preface

Many are the plans in a person's heart,
but it is the Lord's purpose that prevails.
--- Proverbs 19:21 NIV

     This will be the fourth book that I have written, but it probably should have been my first.

     On August 24, 2017, I was involved in a car accident that could have taken a turn for the worse but God spared my life. I suffered a concussion with no internal bleeding, broken bones, or critical injuries. The doctors instructed me to take a break from doing any work, watching television, listening to music, reading, or anything that is mind-stimulating. Everyone close to me was concerned that I wouldn't be able to do it. Anyone that knows me is well aware of how busy I am 24/7. I am dedicated to every area of my life – family, school, work. My mom took my phone but later in the day, she let me speak with two of my mentors over the phone.

     First, my pastor, Rev. Dr. William E. Flippin Sr. who encouraged me to remain optimistic and not to allow that experience to stop me from moving forward towards my destiny. Next, I spoke with a mentor who I truly admire and respect, Dr. Bernice A. King, who reminded me that angels were with me in the time of the accident, encouraging me to listen to the doctors' orders and to take this time out to listen to the voice of God. I am very grateful to God for my family and especially my mother, who made sure I did just that.

Quite frankly, those days of recovery were some of the best days of life that I had in a long time. I was able to focus on the things that mattered, starting with the word that consistently rammed the back of my mind from the moment I started my recovery process: "PURPOSE".

It brought my mind back to four months prior in April when I took a trip to Los Angeles and while there visited Kyle Dendy, a close friend of mine who is a young minister, life coach and author. We went to lunch to catch up on life and ministry but ended up engaging in a quite captivating conversation about purpose. It was so grand that it led to us to going live on Facebook so others could hear and get involved. Kyle and I talked over the span of months about starting an organization that would be solely focused on helping the next generation of leaders discover and drive their purpose. Because we came to the conclusion that there are several institutions of different sorts that teach destiny, life skills, even productivity — but very few, if any, that focuses just on purpose.

This is a problem that I felt could use a solution. Many people spend their entire life trying to discover their purpose and others die never discovering it. I decided at a young age that this cannot be me. I meet people all over the world who are successful in their own respective rights and fields; they're wealthy, they're notable, but they don't know their purpose. And if they do know their purpose, maybe they're not living in their purpose or empowering their purpose. It's more common than you may think because things like wealth, notability, opportunity, legacy do not always equate to purpose discovery or activation.

One month after my accident, I celebrated my 20th birthday. I am grateful that in my young life I have had the opportunity to spend extensive amounts of time around purpose-filled and purpose-led individuals who taught and instilled in me what purpose looks like, how it best operates, and in what ways God's purpose and our purpose intersect one another for a unique, balanced alignment with our destiny and God's will.

I wrote this book because it's time that I share what I've learned over the years from my experiences and lessons in several capacities that I'm confident will enhance the lives of many. This book is for every person who wants to soar into a new season of success in their life and release their destiny. You reading this book is sowing a seed into your life that will reap a harvest of new opportunities, new joy, new understanding, new peace, and new direction.

This book is not for perfect people. The Lord and his purposes are perfect, but we are not. We are unintentionally and sometimes unconsciously assaulted by doubts, fears, uncertainties that very often keep us from living out the purposes that God has established for us. However, we can overcome the adversities in our world, strengthen our faith, reach our potential and accomplish great purposes in God's name.

Sometimes our lives can get so busy and we can focus on so many things that we feel perfectly belongs on our priority list. It is very easy to be driven by the demands of life. Not very often do many of us sit back and ask ourselves: "What is my purpose?" "Am I living according to my purpose?" "Am I empowering my purpose?"

Well, before we get started along the journey to empowering our purpose, I want you to take note of this about purpose, alone:

1. God's Purpose not only encompasses our lives but the lives of those around us
2. God has a purpose for everyone
3. God's purpose is the one that lasts
4. God's purpose can't be undone
5. Every person is born with purpose
6. Unless you empower your purpose, you will never build a legacy

Introduction

It is no coincidence that you have come to find this book, for it was arranged to be this way. There is information and inspiration in this book that undoubtedly will unlock your potential and release your destiny. In fact, you have come here as an act of destiny. This is a time of destiny for you.

Remember, you were made for greatness, not mediocrity. The previous book I wrote, *WALKING IN VICTORY*, astutely attests to this. "We are not human beings having a spiritual experience, but we are spiritual beings having a human experience." As spiritual beings entombed in a human body, we were formed in the image and likeness of the creator – a God of purpose.

It is Heaven's plan for you to maximize your life by aligning your destiny, God's will, and purpose together.

You deserve to be successful and though you should dwell with the spirit of humility, you should not dwell with the spirit of complacency. One of the biggest failures people make is to settle for what is out there. Your dreams and aspirations, your goals, are worth fighting for. It's time to unleash the genius within you and fearlessly fulfill your destiny. You may only be one person but please believe me when I say that there is a vital part that you play in society's upbringing; its advancement into our global destiny.

In case you haven't noticed, this world is evolving. Terms such as "easy" and "normal" have taken on new meanings. This generation has embraced innovation through means of technology and compliance with new social orders. It has caused us all to raise the standard. But, it starts with us making the deliberate decision to evolve and play a part in raising the consciousness of humanity.

Wherever you are in your life right now, God wants to take you higher and I want to help you get there. I want to help you hold on to that unique treasure of your purpose and step into your unique power and position as a conscious creator. It's time to achieve success and release your destiny.

Before we move further in this conversation, it is important that I point out that there is a difference between purpose and destiny, though many fail to recognize it. We often use the terms "destiny" and "purpose" quite interchangeably or in replacing the other the same way we use "vision" and "goals" interchangeably without giving much thought to it. We do it as though they are identical or equivalent, when they are not even similar – they just are all high on the priority list for highly successful entities, people especially.

Destiny should drive purpose, purpose drives action. Destiny is not directly connected to your achievements; that's purpose. Purpose brings clarity to short term expectation, greater focus; while destiny on the other hand brings perspective and direction from a long-term, broader point of view. Both destiny and purpose are uniquely inextricably bound to one another as concepts, as well as its inclusion within the personalities of successful individuals.

What does it mean to empower your purpose? It means to live consciously and intentionally. It means to become the most magnificent version of yourself there is. This happens through the achievement of success by expanding your natural skills and achieving life transformations that push the boundaries of possibility.

Upon the culmination of reading this book, you will have fully visualized your purpose and empowered your life, which will ultimately change your world.

Here is how:

KEY #1 - DO AND DARE
KEY #2 - BE CONSISTENT
KEY #3 - BE TRANSPARENT
KEY #4 - BE HUMBLE
KEY #5 - COMMIT TO EXCELLENCE
KEY #6 – CENTER YOUR BALANCE
KEY #7 – KEEP YOUR FOCUS

KEY #1 - DO AND DARE

Go After Your Vision

I was taught to be modest and humble. But, I was also taught to believe in myself, chase after my dreams, and never allow anything to stop me from pursuing the success that I have envisioned for myself. As much motivation as I had around me from people and confirmations along the road to success, I somehow gauged how to make way on my own. Some call it "encouraging yourself". Others call it "being your own best friend". It is definitely not a matter of isolation or annihilation. It is a matter of believing in yourself regardless of the influence of who, what, when, why, and how.

Ones success in going after your vision is rooted in your basic belief in the reality that you can do just about anything that you set your mind to. It's not cliché that "the sky is the limit". Forget any aspect of your life that is working against your vision coming to past - time, baggage, money, drama, opinions. Invalidate their authority so that the motive of success can take precedence over your present and lead you to a thriving future.

Going after your vision starts with the public and private admittance of three statements:

1. I am destined for more than where I am right now
2. I refuse to be the same, live the same, and   produce at the same capacity than in the past   and in the current.

3. I am ready to enlarge my territory, increase my capacity, and experience my overflow.

These statements are reprimands against complacency, negligence, depression, and any nugatory force that has attempted or continues to derail your train to success. Until you say this and genuinely in your heart become dissatisfied with dissatisfaction, you will never come into contact with your increase. The words of your mouth must match the sincerity of your heart to move forward.

Are you ready experience "greater" in your life? It's time to go after your vision and make the decision today to rid yourself of contrary practices and presences in your life that are preventing you from expediently pushing into to greatness.

Ask yourself these right questions:

1. Do you ever compare yourself to others?

I know social media makes it look like entrepreneurship is easy. Social media makes it look like the lives of the most troubled are easy - leaping over bounds of constant opportunity, limited opposition, and creative expressions of love, joy, and peace. Many of us follow accounts of popular users and even friends to which we feel as though through our following of these accounts, we know their life story. But, social media is not real. The internet is not authentic. And that's not at all to say that the internet is full inauthentic information or that an entity's social media accounts don't reveal authentic information but it is very much to say that what we see online about a person's life is only measured at face value. This can even apply to one's experiences with people in person.

Let's face it – it's hard not to compare yourself to others, especially if people are always sharing their life's experiences with you. It gives you something to compare yourself to. But, it is important that you remember that because you are not that person, you simply do not know the whole story.

The tendency to compare oneself is often linked to ones' underestimation of what they are capable of. Outstandingly, these are typically those who excel in intelligence and creative ability. Comparing yourself to others is dangerous because for the most part all you will ever see is good. Think about it — how many people are willing to expose their "dirty truths".

Focus on you. One thing that is and will forever be unique to you is your story and your journey. No one can ever live your life the way you have and are living your life. You should not compare your beginning to someone else's middle.

Embrace what makes you different. If you focus on you, perfect your best character, and master your craft, you will see that there will be no other person on this earth who can do what you do. Only you can do it like you.

2. How often do you fuel your body?

Ever since I can remember, one thing I have always taken for granted is my stature in height and weight. I am skinny and never have actually gained weight. Honestly, I've probably been 100-105 pounds for the past 4 years and I'm 20 years old. It is amazing that no matter how much I eat or what I eat, from full meals to junk food or desserts, I simply do not gain weight. People would joke when I was little and say all of the time that food I eat goes straight to my big head.

When I was younger I took gymnastics, and made it pretty far up in the rankings. When my schedule became busier than normal, I could not keep up with the practices. I also was heavily in martial arts. Most people do not even know that I have a black belt. Entering into high school, I stopped martial arts and gymnastics, focused on my studies, extracurricular activities and my social life. Everything seemed to be going so great without it just as things were with it.

As far as I was concerned as long as I didn't gain any weight and was not sick, there was no need for me to exercise. I thought I was in good shape. That's until I got to college.

I did not realize I was actually not fit. I had good stamina and if I would randomly do an activity that involved quick physical exercise, I was always able to keep up.

I didn't see what I was missing out on until after watching a television interview about mind, body, and soul on the OWN Network, I decided to fit a daily workout in my schedule. As busy as I was, I figured out how to fit 15 minutes of working out into the beginning of my day in the morning. I felt absolutely amazing. That 15 minutes is now 1 hour.

My one hour workout somehow pumps energy through me that keeps me going throughout the day and helps me experience the most out of it. I came to realize because I worked out at the beginning of the day and took little to no naps throughout the day, not only was I more productive but when it was time for me to sleep, I was more restful than before.

I used to nap throughout the day in quarters. I thought with my constant traveling, meetings, speaking engagements, naps were helping. Little did I know it was interrupting my sleep pattern and caused insomnia. All of this seemed to change from my new workout routine.

This is how I fueled my body. It is important that you figure out what ways you could and will fuel your body. Do not take advantage of your good health or not pay attention to bad health. It can be keeping you stuck and holding you back. I thought that good health was the perfect excuse for not eating as healthy as I could or exercising at all. What I failed to recognize was that getting healthy and feeling good from the inside as well as on the outside are the keys to expansion and growth.

If you want to expand and grow, get out there and move.

3. How do you focus on self-care?

It is so easy to get caught up with ourselves, our ambitions. For many successful people, once they get a taste of success and see how it operates in their lives, they don't stop to take care of themselves. You cannot depend on other people to take care of you. Once you reach a certain stage of independence in your life, self-care is a self-administered amenity that external entities can assist and direct but not necessarily implement.

We are told all of the time to treat others like we want to be treated with dignity, care, respect, but the big question is how often do we apply this golden rule to ourselves? It is unfair to ourselves if we expect people to treat us with dignity, care, and respect if we aren't in the habit of doing it ourselves. Self-care can include what we talked about earlier with exercise to as simple as arranging "you" time. This is most important because it is that time where you are not paralleling with work, work, and work!

We often forget to care for ourselves. We're taught to treat others nicely and with respect, but we don't do it for ourselves. How can we ever expect anyone to treat us well if we can't? Self-care can include a range of things, including exercise and health, a digital detox, scheduling "you" time to do absolutely nothing, bubble baths and grooming. Putting yourself first is not a crime. It's a necessity. Take care of yourself so you can take care of those around you. (P.S. Don't forget to schedule it or it might never get done.)

4. Do you have a daily routine of any sort?

Having a daily practice, a routine that gets you in sync with yourself — your mind and/or your body — and aligns you with your intentions, is key for tapping into your power and strength. It reminds you why you are here and sets the stage for calmness in the midst of daily chaos.

My daily practice consists of guided meditation and gratitude. I wake up very early in the morning daily and pray for everyone on my prayer list and then pray for myself. To follow that is meditation and scripture reading. Yours can include things such as yoga, reading, EFT or prayer. Whatever works to get you feeling good and centered can be made into a habit. Why not start your day with a positive outlook?

5. What role does the opinions of others play in your life?

So many colleagues, friends and clients struggle with this need to please everyone around them. I come from a loving home where gratefully my parents gave me one of the best gifts: freedom of expression. Not only did not parents remind me constantly that I could be all that God destined me to be, but with freedom of expression I was graced with the wonderful opportunity of feeling comfortable with my own thoughts, beliefs, and standpoints on issues, topics, and other realities. It is sometimes so easy to feel guilt every time someone you really care about and respect does not agree with you. You can put so much weight on their opinions and expectations and unconsciously and unintentionally abandon your own.

Your thoughts matter. Your opinions matter. And quite frankly, if no one else believes your opinion or has faith in your opinion, you should. It's time to start thinking for yourself. It's time to start putting your needs first. The only person that has to live your life is you. You deserve to be happy with it and everything that it encompasses.

6. Do you really believe in yourself?

You are only going to run in a few number of people in your life who will have unconditional love for you. But, if you are not one of them there is a problem. You have to be your biggest lover. You are the guide for how everyone around you views you and treats you. The better you treat you, the better others will treat you. It's not mythical dogma. It's the truth.

If you don't find yourself to be worthy of respect and dignity, there is no real reason why anyone else should. You must set the standard for how you want to show up, how you want to feel and how you want to live. Know it. Believe it with every fiber of your being. Believe in you and the amazing gifts you have to share with the world. After all, he gave it to you and no one else. No one's gift is the same, even if it may look like it. This is why God is depending on you to let your light shine and not be ashamed of what you're capable of.

Do not underestimate you. Your vision is worth fighting for; it's worth chasing after.

Whether in the short term or the long-term, your vision is what you plan for, work, for, live for. Every breath that you breathe is for the realization of this vision. The decision to passionately chase after your vision is tied to blatant and deliberate refusal to go one day without doing the very best you can to get closer to it. The power of a vision is in its possibility of becoming a reality because whether it takes 6 months or 6 years, it is something that you actually plan and work for. Dreams can be built overnight, but the realization of visions, on the other hand, are delivered in seasons.

Chasing after your vision is not only a deliberate decision but a deliberate outlook. You have to look at yourself as a professional entity.

Whether you own a business or not, YOU ARE A BUSINESS and you have to treat yourself like it. In order for you to go after your vision, you have to create your life plan, like you would create a business plan. Create your life plan unique to the functions and elements of your life and everything that it encompasses. You own your life. You are responsible for handling the challenges of selling, delivering, financing, managing and growing your life as a business.

Taking up your life as a business involves you being very strategic in behaving ethically and legally. Your ultimate goal is to deliver results of sustained stream of joy, peace, opportunity, and spiritual stability.

It's time you create vision statement. This is what it needs to include:
- Your Dream
- Your purpose
- Beliefs, stands and values
- What you desire for yourself
- Legacy you want to leave
- Who you want to be

Your vision statement can be as long as you want it to be or as short as you want to be. It needs to be written in the present tense. Use words like "I am" not "I will".

Wake up every morning and repeat this vision statement like you own it because it is yours.

Celebrate every gift and talent.

Let's face it – there are some things in life you will not accomplish. The only reason why is because there are millions of things you CAN accomplish in life possibly. God's plans for your life can change in the twinkling of the eye. Some things you don't have time to accomplish because there are only so many hours in a day, days in the week, weeks in the year. You may go after something with every confidence that you can achieve it, and then something unexpected prevents you.

BUT, You have to remember that you are standing in the land of no excuses. So, get rid of these:

-I don't have time (It's not true. We all have time. Everyone has the same 24 hours in the day. 7 days in the week. 365 days in the year. What you do with that time is what matters. This is what separates the successful from the unsuccessful)

-I can't afford my dream. (Do not believe the myth that it takes money to make money. It takes a vision, a good work ethic, and strong communication to make money)

-I'm not good enough (What makes anyone "good enough"?)

-It's too difficult. (We make things harder on ourselves)

Take action and keep moving forward. Focus on action. The journey is not going to always be easy or fun. Failure will come but with delicacy, planning, preparation and consistency, you can set out to do whatever you set your mind to do.

After all that has been said, if you are reading and this and saying to yourself "I guess but…" it is my challenge for you to rid yourself of this in your vocabulary. There are plenty of "nay's", shortcomings, limitations – for everybody. Millions of things you are capable of.

Through the proper conveyance of your dreams, hard work, and consistency ---- you have everything it takes within you and all the resources you need around you. Nowadays you can google just about anything and have access at the tip of your fingers. Mentors are there.

Now that you know the vision, what's next for you?

Double Your Failure Rate

Successful businessman Thomas J. Watson once said: "Would you like me to give you a formula for success? It's quite simple, really. Double your rate of failure. You are thinking of failure as the enemy of success. But it isn't at all. You can be discouraged by failure or you can learn from it, so go ahead and make mistakes."

If you don't know who Thomas J. Watson is, he was the first president of IBM and is remembered to this day as one of the most innovative business leaders of the 20th century. Today, IBM stands as a general in technology. I will tell you it's quite amazing when you can have a legacy that lives on past what you create in the present.

You've heard it a million times that failure is a part of the process to success. It's practical versus just ideal. At the end of the day, God's will for your life is not failure. It is to overcome. So, if you believe in yourself and the authority that the fruition of your dreams holds in your life, you will go after every aim, every aspiration without the negative considerations of what failure can do to you.

Keep failing. Keep succeeding. There is a ratio that no one can seem to finitely figure out, however it's essentially true that the more you aim and fail, the greater leads you have to success.

It's amazing that everyone wants to live a successful life, but we want to do it by being as careful as possible and avoiding failure at every crossroad. Failure is an important part of our equation for success. If you do not fail enough, you may not ever achieve "real" success.

Culture and society has programmed us to believe that failure is bad. It starts in school, you get disciplined and reprimanded if you fail. Then throughout adolescence and our teenage years, we are told so many stories of people who "messed up". We are scared to death about failing. Many of us, believe it or not, operate out of the fear of failing. Even on our jobs, we are reprimanded by our bosses and managers if you make a mistake. In fact, of course, in some cases mistakes can be so heavy-duty, it can lead to our termination. All of this has caused us to believe that failure is bad. But, failure is a good thing.

We should try to change our beliefs about failure and look at it as something good. It is something essential that will ensure our success in both our professional and personal lives.

There are several reasons why failing is crucial to your success. But, here are a few:

1.) Experience and Understanding Can Be Gained by Failure

I know we live in a serious world and we're told once we get to a certain age to toughen up, stand up tall and "don't take any mess". So, we resist failure even when it comes. Some people end up feeling miserable when they can't get something done or when things don't go their way. If they win and are victorious, they celebrate; if they fail, they deliberate on what went wrong. It's that moment of wondering what went wrong and exactly how that you become better, more understanding, all because you have gained a sense of experience.

2.) Failure Takes Your Character to the Next Level

I was in an organization in high school called Future Business Leaders of America, aka FBLA. I served in my senior year as the North Metro Area Vice President for the state of

Georgia. Throughout the year, as a state officer team, we traveled all over the country with our state adviser, Monty. Our trips were consistently entertaining because Monty kept us laughing. I'll never forget some years ago, as a team we went to Washington DC and literally went to every monument in DC in 30-degree weather within a matter of probably 2 hours. I'm from the south so me and cold weather just do not get along. Once it gets below 65 degrees, it's intolerable for me. So, not only were we freezing cold but we were exhausted walking in DC taking train after train, going turn by turn following Monty on his creative tour. Myself and a couple of others would complain and he said one thing that did not really mean a whole lot back then but means a whole lot today. He said "Keep going. It builds character". That became his saying he'd remind us whenever we'd complain about anything throughout the year.

Developed character is irreplaceable. Money can't buy it.
Only experience can provide opportunity for your character to go to the next level, but specifically experiences with failures. Every successful person I know personally and professionally has failed over and over and over again. They have a high failure rate, even still to this day as business owners, millionaires, actors, authors, speakers. But it builds their characters. It gives them the opportunity to learn from their mistakes and come back stronger than they were before they entered into the trial to test their agility.

There is no greater way to reach deeper within you and understand yourself like never before than for you to fail.
Failure keeps things in perspective. You reflect a different kind of way when you fail. Your maturity is saturated when you fail.

3.) Failure Gives You Direction

The decisions that you make is obviously the biggest contribution to your success and anyone's success. As much education and knowledge you think you have, without experience, you're relying on nothing but advice and untested knowledge to determine which decisions are good and which are bad. The experience comes from bad discernments and failures. Difficulties are going to come but you have a choice to either ignore it, give up or you can learn from the situation to get to the right path.

Failure gives you direction. It teaches you the right way, just like a baby when she's first learning how to walk. She's going to fall over and over again but she's going to get it perfectly right the more she tries and fails. She will know in what ways to balance right the next time for that to work. Just because the baby falls a few times while getting up to talk doesn't mean you should stop her from walking because then she would never learn to walk. Instead, you should encourage the baby trying. Keep going at it until she learns for herself.

We should look at the failures of life the same way. You should not look at failures as detriments but as opportunities of opinion that will help navigate you forward.

Now, that you understand the importance of failing, let's talk about how to deal with your failures. This is important because if you do not know how to deal with your failures, it can lead to confusion, depression, and missed opportunities.

1.) Accept failure for its normalcy

Everyone is born a winner in the end. But failure is a part of the process. Accepting the normalcy of failure helps you learn from your mistakes, adjust your strategies and improve to achieve the success that you want for yourself.
Failure is a reminder that you are human and that you are being productive. In its essence, failure is a conduit to help you figure out exactly what is not working right and what is

the better way than before so you can eventually figure out the best way.

2.) Learn From Your Failures

It is meant for you to learn from your failures versus looking at them as some type of ultimate defeat. Failure is feedback, used as a basis for improvement. Your life does not end at the moment that you fail at anything and no matter how much you fail, because there is always something more for you to learn, it makes room for failure to be applicable in the future. If you foster failure correctly, you can see to it its lead to your inevitable best self.

Your rejections and failures in life should motivate you because they do not define you. The most successful people in the world were rejected and failed but they never allowed that to shatter their dream. They train hard. They change their methodology. They move forward with diligence and delicacy until they have accomplished their overarching goal.

3.) Gain Your Strength and Get Back to It

Have no doubt about it that even though rejections and failures are not the end for you, they can inflict a decent bit of pain. We cannot stop there. After you have accepted the failure and learned from it, turn your weaknesses into strength and come back stronger by doing things differently. Make the intentional decision that you will not quit and that your eyes, ears, and heart are open to learn.

Your past is a gateway to your future but remember that your past does NOT equal your future. Failure does not necessarily have to be a part of your life forever because there will come a point where your journey has reached maturity and you've grown in distinct wisdom. If you fail now, it does not mean that you are going to fail again in the future. If you really pull from the pain you felt and maximize its reverberation to meet its your best strength. Your best strength is tied to best skills and best knowledge.

Gain your strength and go back to it so you can accomplish more.

The fact of the matter is that failure is important. This is why you should double your failure rate. I learned at a young age and at the earlier stages of my ministry and my business that the earlier I fail, the faster I learn and improve.

It is wonderful to be careful in life but be careful not to be too careful. Do not wait until you are 40 or 50 years old to make mistakes. You still need energy to get back up again and move forward. The younger you are and you chase after your vision without avoiding mistakes, the more energy you have to recover and get to where you are trying to be. Take as many actions as possible. Double your failure rate. Triple your failure rate. Quadruple your failure rate. At some point, you are going to get it right and by that time you will have reached expert status.

Thomas Edison once said: "I HAVE NOT FAILED. I'VE JUST FOUND 100,000 WAYS THAT WON'T WORK".

You will accomplish more when you have made more attempts to try new things. The faster you fail, the faster you will learn. The faster you learn, the faster you will reach the success you want.

Stretch Your Capacity

Success cannot be universally defined. Everyone has their own definition of what success is. For some, success is becoming notable among family and friends. Success, for some, is becoming notable among a particular industry they are involved in. For some, success is becoming notable before the world. Success, for others, is a matter of making a certain amount of money or reaching levels that their parents and ancestors did not get to. Then, there are those who can find success in solely their happiness and peace.

Regardless of what you find success to be, you will never receive it until you have distinctly defined success for yourself. What do you want out of life? How much do you want from life?

I want you to stop for a moment right now and think about the one thing you want your life to stand for; that one thing you want your life to mean to you and others. I want you to think about what it means for you to live a fulfilling and extraordinary life. If there was a door that would lead you to that very thing, would you open it, even if there was some pain that you would inflict to get there?

You see, becoming safe along your journey is not a matter of avoiding failure and "being realistic" as some would say. You become safe when you have set your goals and delicately and deliberately put them in action.

Your life, as a business, and even your business itself, if you are an entrepreneur, will only improve when you stretch your capacity, going over the cliff even if you risk instability. That is when true growth happens.

Step Out of Your Comfort Zone

Admit it – comfortable feels good, so we tend to lean towards it. Whenever we are in an uncomfortable space, we do everything we can to move out of it and get into a space that is normal and most familiar to us. This is best known as our comfort zone. It is good to know what our comfort zone is but it is a terrible thing to solely bask in it and never step out because growth does not happen inside the comfort zone. If you want to be more successful in business, relationships, and life, you have to step outside of your comfort zone and meet a challenge that faces you head on.

    Stepping out of your comfort zone is not a bad thing. You are not relinquishing your personal values or anything as to that nature. It is risky to step out of your comfort zone because several things could happen. You could come to face your true self: your insecurities, shortcomings, true weaknesses, real strengths, and the list goes on and on. The most intense thing you may face will be the risk of failure, which, if you double your failure rate, will create a forced necessity for you to make an even greater effort to succeed. At this point, you will have too much to lose when you have laid everything you have on the table.

    I used to have a big problem with stepping out of my comfort zone because, not only was I most comfortable with where I was and how I was, I felt that it was keeping me afloat. Little did I realize that it was holding me back. For as long as I can remember, since I started preaching at the age of 5, I have always been a quite serious person. I only engaged in certain spaces with specific people. I stayed to myself.

    Now, don't get the wrong idea. I was not an introvert or a socially awkward person but I simply did not know how to have fun and when those opportunities for fun came, I could not figure out how to make it work for me.

    I was so serious that when I would get into spaces with powerful and influential people who noticed how serious I seemed to be in even the most casual settings like their homes and at other social gatherings, they would ask me "Why are you so serious all of the time?"

It wasn't until I graduated from high school that I realized that I stayed in a bubble of career fluency. People told me ever since I was little that I had an "old soul" or that I was an old man in a young man's body. I do remember at some point when I was very young taking offense to that because I felt that people were belittling me for my stature. Little did I know that they were really just trying to make sense of why my personality was so profound and solemn. I dealt with a lot of criticism growing up from people and media saying that I was sheltered by my family, when really that has never been true. My mom and dad always wanted me to get out and have fun, invite friends over the house – LIVE!

Stepping out of my comfort zone for me was a decision to have fun. Yes, that meant getting out of the house for more than just church, family gatherings, meetings, and networking events. At some point, I had to remind myself that there is a world out there full of people and things to do. I had to remember that my parents raised with values that were instilled since I was a young boy and was nurtured through my adolescence as I became a young man that was going to keep me grounded in truth and morale. But, not only that, I had to believe that God wanted me to live outside of the church and business.

The day I decided to step outside of my comfort zone is the day that I noticed God beginning to open up unexpected doors and unimaginable ways were made.

Normal and familiar is not always best. Things happen in life and sometimes you may need to slow down and decelerate, but whatever you do – keep moving forward. Set sporadic milestones and do not be satisfied until you have reached a new level.

I meet so many people on a daily basis with potential out of this world but they let fear get the most of them. They feel as though they are inadequate, unknowledgeable or simply not able. Fear has no place in the heart and soul of the determined. I challenge you today to overcome fear and decide to step out of your comfort zone so you can grow and progress. If you want to see real results, you need to step outside your comfort zone.

Stretch Yourself Frequently

A one-time stretch is useless. God never enters us into a dimension for us to bask in forever. He wants us to grow. I believe that one of the greatest spirits we unconsciously fight is the spirit of complacency, where we feel smug or develop uncritical satisfaction with ourselves and our achievements. Stretching yourself must be a constant activity. This is important because after you have stretched yourself, your comfort zone changes to where you have transitioned to be.

You see, the more you stretch yourself, the more your comfort zone expands. You have to keep stepping outside of your comfort zone so you can keep moving forward in business and life. It is easier than you think to become stagnant because success has a good way of slowing us down once we have started to experience a little bit of it. You know how that is – we grow up with dreams and goals and once things start to fall in place and make sense, we don't move with the same agility that pushed us to do more than what we imagine because what we think has now already aligned with what we see to be possible.

As soon as you have conquered one challenge, you have to set a new one. Do not be satisfied with small victories. These are great and important, and you do need to set achievable goals but there are more goals on the prospect list that you have to look at.   Even the word "achievable" does not have to be small, obvious and easily tangible. If you want to start your new company to become a Fortune 500 corporate entity, that is achievable. If you have a book on the inside of you that you are going to write and get published and launch to the top of the NY Times Bestseller list, that is achievable. If you want to be a blockbuster movie star or a chart-topping, Grammy Award winning artist, that is achievable.

Just because something is slightly or outstandingly out of your reach does not negate the possibility of it becoming yours to touch and grab hold of.

Even though stretching myself opens me to the possibility of failure, I do it anyway. I constantly stretch myself, even if it does not guarantee a delivery of a lead or a specific opportunity. If I stretch for 30% growth in my business and "only" hit 25% growth, that is still a win for me. I can reset and work toward that 30% goal again. All of the goals that you choose to set for your business, life, and even relationships with friends, colleagues, and significant others can fall into this simplistic, beneficial model.

The reality is that you will not hit the ball park each time, but that really is not the point. The point is that you improve each day. Because I made the decision a while back to stretch myself frequently, I find myself to become a better person each day. I am increasing my capacity. I am creating possibility of growth and learning. I am challenging myself to reach for goals that are outside of my comfort zone, yet still attainable, but setting myself up to accomplish true amazing things.

Note that this is something that only you can do. It does not matter how much money you have to offer or power to lend. No one will work as hard for you than you.

Here are 6 things you can do to stretch yourself:

1) Develop a new reading list.

As a preacher, student and steward, I have always been fond of personal development/self-help/leadership books. My library is full of books by John Maxwell, TD Jakes, Dave Ramsay, Joel Osteen and other authors of those likings. But, just reading these types of books are not stretching myself. So, I chose some years ago to diversify my library, reading more fiction books, history books, relationship books, even cooking books.

You want to read something different from what you normally read. If you like to read nonfiction books like me, pick up a fiction book and switch it up. Maybe you're like me and you're not too fond of comic books or books that have long storylines for me to follow, do it anyway. It makes you more versatile.

2) Get some friends who are not like you.

That's right. Remember that law of attraction: you attract you are and you are who you attract. It's applicable but, in this case, it grows on you. I did not start to grow until I started to hang around people who were not into the exact same things that I am into. My friend group is so diverse with different personalities and interests. I have friends who are outwardly exuberant and others who are quiet. I have friends who are churchy and others who do not go to church at all. I have friends who are both conservative and liberal, some who are leaders and others who are managers, some who are thinkers and others who are shakers.

There is only one type of person who is not included in my friend group and these are "still people". We all know at least one person who fits in this category. Stay away from "still people": still complaining, still hating, still losing, still broke, still not making a change, still living in the past, still making excuses. Expand your friend group and make some changes to them if they do not currently fit along your journey of traveling to where God really wants you to be. No matter how hard you try, there are some people who do not deserve to be in your friend group because they are not improving themselves and limiting you from stretching yourself.

3. Try to do something you have never done.

What are you good at? What can you do? Now, think beyond that – and do it. That's right. Just do it. Forget about the risks attached and make it happen. Take that class. Learn that language. Play that instrument. Ask that girl out. Try out for that team. That "it"; the more different you are from it – the greater the stretch. That is what it is all about.

4. Do not waste your time on problems and planning.

Too many people reach out to me with amazing ideas and dreams that seem to never come into fruition. You would be surprised how many people spend so much time planning and mapping out their solutions to anticipated or present problems versus just doing it. A lot of this is because the world has a very unique way of weighing us down and discouraging us. We cannot avoid the current problems in our lives or the problems to come, but we can discipline ourselves to focus more energy towards advancement rather than repair. Try it. In my experience, every event I have organized and program I have launched – sure I took the time to do simple research and analysis to make sure that I was not getting into anything that would significantly affect me. But, I was not going to spend too much time focusing on what could go wrong or the tedious pieces of work versus just getting it done.

5. Stay mentally and physically active.

If you really want to be successful, your mental and physical stamina has to be on another level. I mention staying physically active as well as mentally active because you stretch your mind when you stretch your body. And the more you stretch your body, the more you stretch your mind. Keep moving and doing things that stimulate your mind to think and go.

6. Move Forward even when it does not make sense.

Uncertainty is everywhere and you are not going to be able to get rid of its presence anytime soon in your life. When you are making decisions, very rarely will you have all of the answers in front of you. But, what is faith if we have all the answers and we know every single thing? It is time for you to take a new risk on something even if it does not make all of the sense in the world. It is how you stretch yourself and move forward.

Build Self-Confidence Through Taking Action

I believe that at some point and in some particular area, each of us have had our share of experiences with self-confidence. That is not to say that you did not believe in yourself but it is to say that maybe you believed in yourself in one area but not in the other; or maybe it was that you felt liberated in one area and bound in another.

Some of you reading this are currently having confidence issues. Do you wake up in the morning believing that you are the best you that exist? Do you feel as though you are good enough, handsome enough, pretty enough, smart enough, or most of all <u>achieved</u> enough? Do you get intimidated when you are around people who inspire you?

Here are some specific actions that you can take to reach new levels of confidence in your life

1. Remember names.

It seems minor and unnecessary, but it is not. When someone introduces themselves to you, repeat their name one time and if possible twice in the conversation. Write it down in the notes section of your phone along with a quick note as to where you met them. Before you go to sleep that night, recount all of the important names of the people you met and you will high likely never forget a name again.

2. Dress your best and the part

Before you can dress your best, you have to accept that your perspective of "best" may not be "the best" if comparatively, criticism is true. Dressing your best is not about how much you spend on clothes but the pride in how you look. My mom used to always tell me when I was little to always take pride in how you look. I paid it no mind until I got older and realized that spending those extra minutes on grooming and clothes, showing diversity, fully accessorizing outfits, and coinciding with current trends actually work. When you look better, you feel better. Look like the part you want to play. Suit up for success. Your clothes and your accessories should make way for your personality to shine. Instead of spending bunches of money on a variety of clothes, focus on bold jewelry, colorful ties, fancy shoes, popping accessories that become focal points to let people know that "you are about business".

3. Give promises and keep them.

Yes, believe it or not, you might give promises that you do not keep. I am not just talking about promises to other people but also promises to yourself. You know, just like when you promised yourself you would give this person a call or make dinner on these days of the week, or be on time to this meeting. If you make genuine promises to yourself, you will stop disappointing yourself because you will have built accountability and confidence.

4. Get Your Money together.

You will never build wealth until you have a wealth plan of action. And yes, it is true that the more money you have in your pocket, the more at ease you feel. It is not that money is the most important thing but it is more so that money can chip away at your confidence if you are broke. Make a plan to be financially stable or become wealthy. Reduce your debt. Set up automatic payments. Reduce your spending. Pay big dividends, long term. Make short-term and long-term investments. Know your credit score and have a plan of action to get to an 850.

5. Research and Read to make you smart.

It sounds simple because it is. What makes someone an expert is someone who has extensive knowledge or ability based on research, experience, or occupation and in a particular area of study. You see, anyone can write a book about anything and technically consider themselves to be an expert at it if they delivered on reach, experience or occupation as it relates to what they are an expert in.

6. Fix the broken things in your life.

Start with what's small, like the things in your house. Broken shower curtain, loose door knob, dripping faucet. Get it fixed to remind yourself that you are in charge and that you are responsible for the complete fixing of the broken item.

7. Learn a new skill.

Learn a new language. Take up a fun challenge. Whatever that skill that you have longed to desire to do – make it happen. You need to feel good about what you can do. The more you grow abilities, the more you grow confidence.

8. Change a habit, for the better.

There are habits I had that I did not know were bad until I was told or discovered the hard way. For example, versus checking my email every 30 minutes, now I check it 3 times a day. Making calls during certain times in the day and handling specific tasks in other areas of the day, drinking and eating less this or that – the list goes on. Think of what that habit is that you need to get rid of and change it.

9. Exercise every day.

You read that right. Every day; not every other day or every week, but every day. Get in the gym and exercise your body. Try exercising every day for at least 20-30 minutes and you will see how that will help you boost your self-confidence. In this case, your body is reflective of the work you put into it. As you begin to see your body change, your attitude towards yourself and your life will be more positive.

10. Pray and Meditate for 10 minutes.

There is nothing wrong with meditation. Meditation can be quite scary because some people think you have to be an expert to meditate but that is not true. Meditation in this sense has everything to do with creating one-to-one time with yourself and your thoughts. You do not have to be sitting down with your legs crossed on a small mat to meditate. You can be walking or sitting in a quiet room. Just take 10 minutes.

11. Avoid avoiding

Avoiding and playing it safe might mean you won't fail, but it also guarantees that you won't succeed! You are much stronger and more capable than what you think and you have to believe that for yourself to fulfill your destiny. It is time for you to do something new and surprise yourself with greatness. To build confidence, you need to experience progress and success and the only way to see that come forth for you is to avoid avoiding.

12. Speak Assertively

This is not about you giving a speech every time you are having a conversation. This is about you speaking confidently, in a steady rhythmic tone. Think before you speak. Avoid "ums" and "ahs". It interrupts the flow. There is nothing wrong with taking pauses. It is not awkward or peculiar to do such. Figure out what that balance is for you between assertive and aggressive. Your style and tone of speaking contributes to your self-confidence. You will feel your self-esteem begin to rise when you speak assertively because people will listen to you more attentively when they see the leader radiate from within you. You will literally command the attention and authority in the rooms that you walk into.

13. Become a great actor

All presenters are actors. Good presenters are conscious of their body language. Your body language can instantly demonstrate self-assuredness or it can scream insecurity. In any situation, you want to be presented as a man or woman of control, not necessarily dominance – because dominance is oppressive. Control is slightly different because it tells everyone around you that nothing happens to you that you are not monitoring. It is that you are taking control of that situation. Hold your head up high, sit all the way straight, bring your shoulders back to align your spine and look directly at the other person when interacting. Shake people's hands with firm grips and keep eye contact at all times when someone is speaking with you. Body language speak volumes more than words.

14. Celebrate your achievement

Whether it is big or small, celebrate it. We have always been good at punishing ourselves for things that have gone wrong, but very few do we thank ourselves for the great things we have done. Every week, treat yourself to something, even if it is an ice cream cone from Ben & Jerry's or a milkshake from SONIC. Make it a point to celebrate what you have accomplished in your life.

15. Always be prepared

Do you remember the 5 P's? Prior planning prevents poor performance. I learned this when I was a kid. The more prepared you are, the more confident you will feel about your expertise and competency. You see, preparation does not necessarily avoid mishaps but it makes mishaps easier to manage and maneuver through. Be prepared in the sense of time, size, etc.

KEY #2 - BE CONSISTENT

Increase Your Productivity

Successful people are consistent in every area of their life. Consistency is a stimulus so it commands a response. Inconsistency is not a stimulus so it does command a response. Now, that is not to say that inconsistent people do not become successful. But, it is to say that if you are aiming for intentional, deliberate success under deliverable terms that you set, consistency must be at the forefront of every single thing you do.
 This is one of the most powerful lessons I feel that I learned over the years. Consistency will always deliver results, regardless of the aim. It is universal law. For the aim of success and destiny, consistency creates limitless opportunity.
Everyone gets the same amount of time in the day: 24 hours, 1,440 minutes, and 86,400 seconds. What you do with that time is up you to.
 It takes a lot to get me mad (and I do mean a lot). I am not a passive person but I do not just get agitated over anything. But, the one thing that I become frustrated about is when people or things waste my time. My time is all I have. I cannot restore my time. I cannot replace my time. When time has been spent, it is time that I simply cannot get back.

Here are some things that you can do to increase your productivity.

1. Track and limit your task management

Technology has made this much easier than my parents and grandparents had to take up when they were my age. If you choose not to take advantage of the amazing technology out there, you are losing out on the opportunity to grow. Studies show that micromanagement works but multitasking does not work. Micromanagement only works when it is visibly measurable. You may think you are pretty good at gauging how much time you are spending on various tasks but unless it is down on paper or in front of you to visualize, you are probably not. Download an app or a desktop software that helps you figure out exactly how much time are you spending on social media, email, word processing, phone calls, proposals, etc.

2. Take regular breaks.

As long as your breaks are scheduled and on the books, it is great for your productivity. It makes sure you are able-minded to be most productive by improving concentration. Breaks do not need to be naps. Naps can sometime take too long, but taking short breaks during long tasks will help you maintain a constant level of performance. If you do not take breaks working at long tasks, you will see a steady decline in performance.

3. Set deadlines and follow them strictly

In our homes and at our jobs, we are faced with plenty of open-ended tasks and projects. Do not be so open-ended that you do not set a specific deadline to tasks. You will be very surprised to see how focused and productive you can be when you are watching the clock and knowing that really there is not all of the time in the world.

Productivity can be mean a lot to different people but for most the part, productivity is producing more. Good productivity is how fast you can get something done, how much you can get done or how capable you are at getting something done. It all depends on your situation and how you work. You know yourself more than anyone else does. You know what works and what does not work. Since everyone is different, there are different approaches to productivity.

The outlook on superb productivity is that you are doing more or getting more done because that is what it literally means to produce. Your time is your money and your money is your time. You have to ask yourself what are you doing with your time and how much are you producing with it? Being productive involves you continuing to do, go and produce, all at the same time, and that, in itself, can be extremely stressful if you have not done it before. This is why most people who are on the verge of success in their own respective right start seeing what it looks like to produce a lot at one time and slow down because they are not too sure as how to manage it.

Multi-tasking does not work and will lead you down a road to less productivity. Many people are busy for absolutely no reason or for the wrong reasons. They call themselves "not having time" when really it is not that they do not have time, they just choose to spend their time on the wrong things. Giants in global leadership like Oprah Winfrey, Mark Zuckerberg, and Bill Gates made their mark in history and took memorable, impactful strides by making best use of the time they had in one day. And even today, I am in these circles with greats as these and the most successful people in the world are masters in time and task management.

Do not focus on being busy. Busy does not always equal productive. Focus on producing more in short or long spans of time. Again, use technology to help you become a master at time and task management. When I show people my calendar, they are shocked because I plan out almost every moment of the day and it has probably been that way ever since the age of 13. From meals to exercise to waking up and going to bed, to meetings, to speaking engagements to slots to make phone calls, slot to send emails, slot to draft proposals and other writings.

I have a lot of dreams, several goals. On top of that, I have several businesses as well as preach, and managing other freelance projects here and there in community activism, coaching/consulting and more. If I did not learn how to master time and task management, my life would be all over the place and quite frankly I would probably get little to nothing done.

You have to figure out what is making you unproductive and destroy the myths about productivity. I can give you an example. Of course, with everything that I was doing in ministry and in business at the age of 10 +, I was handling it out of my home and I convinced myself to believe that I was not being as productive as I could have been while at home and that I needed an office space. So, I went off downtown Atlanta and bought an office space, signing a 12-month lease under the supposition that I was going to produce more, make more money, hire more staff, and take on more meetings. When I moved in, I remember setting up a Staples business account and ordering so much décor, supplies, and technology.

What a big mistake that whole ordeal was. The landlord was nice enough to let me out of the lease after a few months and I realized that I could not afford it. Actually, before I moved into the space, I knew I could not afford it after a few months but I just insisted that things would be different once I moved in. It was not until years later that I actually needed office space.

Possibly, if by that time, I had mastered time and task management and there was a significant need that an office space provided, as it aligned with my current resources, an office space could be useful. But there are several reasons why it created no lead generation. One was that I took on way too many meetings. I owned a management consulting firm, which I still operate today and I thought then that bringing prospective and existing clientele to my office would increase legitimacy and build greater trust. I would literally schedule ten 20-30 minutes daily in person.

These in person meetings took way too much time out of my day and it had to stop. I concluded that the goals and tasks of most of these meetings could be accomplished via email, phone, or via an on-line meeting. By the time I realized this, I was out of an office space because the budget was done over.

The lesson I learned in this novice stage was that you do not have to have a professional office space to be productive. I needed to master time and task management and use all of the resources that I had to produce more.

It is so amazing how we can blame so many circumstances and people in our lives as to why we are so unproductive. We give excuse after excuse after excuse, just like I did with my office space. Simply, be more productive.

Get off of Facebook. Get off of Twitter. Get off of Instagram. They are distractions if they are taking up too much of your time. Be deliberate with the time you spend on social media and put a cap on how much you spend on these outlets. I spend at most 25-35 minutes on social media daily. When I hop on Twitter, I get on there to see what is trending and join the conversation with a tweet. It is a waste of time for me to spend 10 minutes scrolling up and down my timeline to see what else is going on. The same goes with Facebook and Instagram.

Many people are victims of checking your emails too frequently. Unless you work a job that requires you to check your emails every 30 minutes to an hour, it is best to check your emails 3 times a day: once in the morning when you wake up, in the afternoon, and before you to go to sleep. Checking your email more often does not make you more productive. In fact, it can prevent you from getting your work done in other areas. The average person checks their email 30 times a day, which is beyond unnecessary. Not checking your email every few minutes is not about being insensitive, rude, or disrespectful. It is a matter of being productive, getting work done, and not playing silly email games. The decision to check your email less will set expectations from everyone around you and especially those who are emailing you that you are a busy person who values their time and will get back to them soon.

Check it in the morning after you have done your morning routine. Respond to the overnight emails and get the emails you need to send that day out of the way. Instead of stopping in the middle of the day to draft up and write an email, think about the email that needs to be sent throughout the day, write it down in your notes that it needs to be done and do it in your "email-time". Doing this early in the morning makes it easier for you to plan your two other times to check your email out in your head because not only can you respond to others but you can also get delegations out early and get tasks out of your inbox that need to now go on your to-do list.

      Your second time in the day to check your email depends on how far you got along in your first email check. Then comes your last time in the day to check your email which enables you to close the loops and follow-up on those unfinished tasks. Maybe there was something that you needed to address or be delegated. Maybe there was an inquiry sent to you that you did not require an immediate response. Your end of the day check time should also be your moment to plan for tomorrow's email-time. You do not have to feel guilty for not responding to every email within 30 minutes to an hour. There is a reason why more people have your email than they have your phone number. Email is not meant to be an immediate communication method.

      Remember, being productive means to do things intentionally with high production as the end goal. If you have free time in the day, spend that time doing some brainstorming, perfecting your to-do list – these are things that actually matter.

      Make the most use of your time. I would say actually that one of the best ways to make the most use of your time is by giving yourself the most time. That starts by waking up early every morning. You cannot wake up at 10a.m., whether it be a workday or an off day, and expect to have a productive day. You have to consider the several things that hold up work in your day, like eating and commuting. By the time you wake up and get your day going, your day will be over and you will have not gotten done as much as you could have.

      Your best bet is to wake up no later than 6a.m. daily. This gives you enough time to get your day going and get the most out of your day. Wake up in the morning and go exercise. This will get the blood pumping in every way that you need to clear your head and regain your focus.

      Do not allow the phone calls and emails that you receive throughout the day dictate how you spend your day. You will end up spending your days putting out fires and very little will be accomplished. In other words, do not be reactive. Be proactive. Indeed, there are some things that come up in our lives that we have to lend our attention to and unfortunately can divert your schedule a little. Have a plan of attack at the start of each day and then do your best to stick to it.

Even if you are an entrepreneur and you work for yourself, you need to set work hours and differentiate that from off-duty time. As you are trying to figure out what are the best work hours for you, try to get the bulk of your work done in 5 hours per day. Florida State University's research department found that elite performers (athletes, musicians, professionals) who work in intervals of no more than 90 minutes are more productive than those who work 90 minutes-plus. During work hours, turn off notifications. Nothing is worth your productivity and your peace of mind. This is all a part of being proactive rather than reactive. You see it is not about who works the longest and burning yourself but it is all about working smarter.

Speaking of working smarter, not harder. Do not be afraid to ask for help and delegate tasks. It took me 18 years to learn this lesson. Everybody needs help and should never take on big projects, large events, or programs on their own. It does not matter how competent or skillful you are. You are only one person and you must accept that. I know this personally because I am very skillful person. I am great at administration, creative thinking, project management, crisis management, marketing, but I am only one person. When it comes down to getting the most out of what I put in, it will never happen by way of me working with just me alone. I learned that I needed help and the most amazing thing about it is that the help I needed was there all along and extended the olive branch to join the team, join the movement – it was me. I was the hindrance of myself for getting help. It all boiled down to my issues with two areas: trust and introversion.

It was never that I had a hard time trusting people or trusting colleagues who were helping me complete work in the sense of them not keeping anything confidential or something as to that nature. But, it was more so that I had difficulty trusting that they could do what I could do as equal or better than me because I felt that I was the most passionate person for the job. Well, in one sense, I was absolutely right. I was the most passionate person for the job because, remember I mentioned earlier that no one wants what you want for yourself as much as much as you. Yet, as a team, you are better together and people can grow to become passionate about your projected outcome. Give your deadlines, share your resources so you can reach the best deliverables. Keep a positive, strong-suited work circle of thinkers, innovators, movers, and shakers that will not settle for less and have the stamina to keep moving forward. Minimize every interruption to the best of your ability and just take a step back and think about the several ways that you can work smarter, not harder.

Stop watching so much TV. That's right. I said it. What productive person really has time for so much TV? Now, I am a film and television fanatic. I have my favorite TV shows like The Big Bang Theory and Scandal. I can pull up Netflix and have a fun time binge watching shows like Stranger Things and 13 Reasons Why. Even with film, I can watch Tyler Perry movies all day long and kick my feet up to watch Kevin Hart, Taraji P Henson, and other movie stars all day. But I would really have to think how much time of mine is that taking up. Americans spend around 34 hours per week watching television, according to Nielsen. Empires and businesses do not get built on your couch watching television or in your bed chilling with Netflix.

Make things visual for you to see. I went to my first vision board party some years ago hosted by one of my good friends, Mary Pat Hector. It was a phenomenal experience casting this vision by matching it with visuals to see it out. I have always been a visual person and I think that actually most people are. For me, this how I discovered that casting a vision, planning a project, managing my schedule, or keeping up with my tasks list cannot be done in my head if expected to be successful. Google Calendar and Wunderlist are my virtual best friends. They keep me in sync and on track. I know my deadlines for tasks before they arrive. I time them so that I do not lose focus on other items on my to-do list, therefore, nothing gets neglected. Most of all, I can have a sense of accomplishment because I have been given a visualization of progress. Sometimes if we do not cast the vision and write our task lists, we will feel as though we are not progressing when we may very well be doing so.

  Productivity revolves around your time and how well are you doing producing in proportion to your goals and timing. If you lock in productivity as a part of your nature, it will be a total game changer for you. Keep your goals in sight at all times. Know what you want and increase your productivity so you can get there.

Becoming More Effective and Efficient

Efficient vs. Effective – Yes there is a difference. Both equate in significance. To be efficient is to perform or function in the best possible manner with the least waste of time and effort. The difference between effectiveness and efficiency can be summed up shortly, sweetly, and succinctly. Being effective is about doing the right things, while being efficient is about doing things right.

Efficiency is about making the best possible use of resources. Efficient people and entities maximize outputs from given inputs, and so minimize their costs. By improving efficiency, a business can reduce its costs and improve its competitiveness.

Are you familiar with Parkinson's law? It is basically the adage that "work expands so as to fill the time available for its completion". In project management, it is a hack or a tool that mandates for work to expand to fill the time allotted for its completion. Time management, after all, is psychological. We naturally pace ourselves to finish a project in the nick of time. Most people suffer from student syndrome, which essentially is planned procrastination where you only start to apply yourself to an assignment or project at the last possible moment before its deadline, eliminating any potential safety margins and puts you under stress and pressure.

In the 20th century, British scholar C. Northcote Parkinson coined a proverb known as Parkinson's law that has been implemented by quite successful leaders in global society to maximize money and wealth accumulation. Parkinson's Law never fails us in its natural sense but you can violate Parkinson's law. This is when financial independence and entrepreneurial freedom comes. The way the law works is no matter how much money people earn, they tend to spend the entire amount and a little bit more besides. Their expenses rise in lockstep with their earnings. A lot of people earn today 3 times what they were earning at their first jobs that paid good wages. But somehow, they seem to need every single penny to maintain their current lifestyles. No matter how much they make, there never seems to be enough.

Even the most financially savvy fall victim to the applications of this law. It is really a trap and hence, for some, provides reason for debt, money worries and financial frustration. It is only when you develop enough willpower to resist the urge to spend everything you make that you will begin to accumulate money and move ahead of the crowd.

The second piece of Parkinson's Law is "if you allow your expenses to increase at a slower rate than your earnings, and you save or invest the difference, you will become financially independent in your working lifetime." This is powerful because if you can place a wedge in between your growing income and your increasing costs of living, and then save and invest the difference, you can continue to improve your lifestyle as you make more money.

Parkinson's Law is applicable to both time and money interchangeably because your money is your time and your time is your money. Carefully examine every element of time you have and what you choose to do with it, the same you would do with the expenses that you currently take up and figure out ways to economize or cut back at those expenses. In the same sense, figure out ways to make better use of your time. Resolve to save time to lend over to the next day or the next hour or the next moment. Try not to run out of time. Treat your time like you would treat your budget. Save and invest 50 percent of any increase in your time and budget you receive in your income from any source. As time goes by, live on the rest of it.

Violate this law. Make deadlines for everything. No matter how big or small, set the deadline. Finance your life reasonably according to income that makes you comfortable. The law provides great leverage for efficiency. Find what that sweet spot is for you when it comes to having a productive hustle.

Find your flow. An athlete would call it being "in the zone". When you are so focused, you can be numbed out to any distractions and that is the goal. If you are in any type of freelance entrepreneurial entity as an entrepreneur or writer, or musician, where what you put in is what you get out because there is no set salary and so forth, both prolonged work and rushed work can be a recipe for reckless work. The goal is to tap into a state that regardless of what environment we are inhabiting, we can still optimize our performance and see to it the balance between challenge and skill.

Do not go into anxiety and frustration because a task has become too challenging or beyond our skill. Then we fall from being over-challenged to be under-challenged and we deal with things like boredom. Stretch yourself, but do not snap. We are most efficient when we are in our zone.

Focus on one task at a time. As I mentioned before, multitasking simply does not work. Scale back on your projects and switch tasks versus managing several tasks at once. Make sure that it fits in with your circadian rhythm. Nerve cells in our brain control our circadian rhythms, which influences sleep-wake cycles, hormone release, emotions and energy levels. When you operate outside of your circadian rhythm, you create fatigue. Many people get tired easily because they are fighting against what their body is telling them to do.

For example, the first couple of hours after waking up in the morning is the best time to get your analytical work done because when you arise in the morning your body temperature increases blood flow to the brain. Midday is best for strategic and tedious work. After lunch time, you have fallen out of the biological peak time for alertness because the digestive process has sapped your energy. Being mindful is this a step towards taking control of your day.

Another step towards taking control of your day is coming into contact with your willpower. It is like a muscle that not only you can exercise to convince yourself that you can, but you can exercise to remind yourself that you will. Publicly declaring this out of your mouth daily that you will resist temptation, you will stay focused, you will reach more and do more, making you more efficient.

It starts with making a statement out of your mouth that "I will". Follow it with a smile, even if there is realistically nothing to smile about. Our brain is wired to respond to certain physiologies — a forced smile will still release endorphins. Pulling yourself out of a figurative slump is as simple as pulling yourself out of a physical slump.

The world is a competition, one big marketplace. If you want to make your mark, you have to bring innovation to the table and trademark it like none other before anyone else does. Be a team player, congratulate others, but be deliberate or you will suffer from under-communication. Know what you want and have a plan to deliver on your desires.

Pace yourself. Sometimes you have to disconnect from not only the distractions but the good and proactive actions. Social media can have you stuck. Even checking your phone all of the time for a text message or a phone call can add up in a day's worth of time. Get off your phone. Get off your computer. Power down sometimes, go off the grid, go on vacation. Disconnect.

Do not forget to sleep and eat. Yes, I said it because productive people have a tendency of doing this. They hunger success so much; they forget out what is most important. Everyone has their own sleep routine because everyone knows how much sleep they specifically need in order for them to keep going. Fatigue dampens creativity and can marginalize productivity. Give your brain some shelter each night and establish a regular circadian rhythm. Habits such as eating, sleeping, and waking at the same time each day signal the body it's time to work, play, or rest. Waking up bright-eyed and well-rested will boost your mood and naturally lower stress.

    Have self-checks to figure out where you are. Do not slow down; just get a shape up to make sure you know what is next and what lies ahead.

    If you do not do this, you can be expeditiously moving and not be sure if what you are doing is productive. To be clear, productivity levels can always be improved.

    New ideas and maximum efficiency comes out of thought clarity. Having those few minutes every day to simply "be" can help in more ways than you think. You have to get in the habit of training your mind to unwind and reboot, which takes devotion and consistency.

Valuing Your Time

Let me ask you ask you question – Do you value your time?

Your answer is probably yes.

But, before you answer I want you think about the past 24 hours of your life. Think about the people who simply wasted your time. Think about how you let others schedule, interrupt and otherwise squander it at will.

So, I'll ask again do you value your time?

Your actions and behavior convey a different message. When you let others take your time, you are in essence saying that your time isn't valuable. If your time is so precious, why do you let others take it freely? If you are not giving them that time and they are taking it without asking, are they not in essence stealing it?

You value your money and don't let people take it.

You value your home and you don't let people take it.

You value your family and don't let people take it.

It is time for you to do the same with your time. If you are wasting your time, you are wasting your life because your time is all you have. You can get more money. You can buy a new house. You can buy a new car. You can create new memories but one thing you cannot buy is taken time.

Think about the signals you send to people about taking your time:
- Saying yes to every request and favor
- Letting others control your calendar
- Allowing other people's priorities to run your own.

If you do not set expectations about your time, then others will believe that they can take it any time they want.

Regardless of who you are, what you may do, or where you may come from, your time is valuable. Stop giving it away freely to people who do not deserve it.

You cannot say yes to everything that comes your way. I am so grateful that at an early age God gave me two gifts: the gift of "bye-bye" and the gift of "no". I can say those two in a heartbeat. When you have priorities of your own starting with yourself and family, saying no must be a significant piece of your communication to help people realize that you are not someone to be tampered around with. Your goals matter and will be accomplished when you do not say yes to everything.

Nobody or nothing should take control of your day. Interruptions come but do not drop what you are doing unless it takes up extreme importance. Put your focus and attention on the people and tasks in front of you. It is good to be tangible and reachable but not at all times. Do not let people, phones, emails, and more keep you from having more than 3 minutes of concentration. Sometimes you need to shut out the interruptions. Close the door, turn off the phone and email. Maybe just schedule some quiet time with your important work. Remember, your phone is there for your convenience, not theirs.

Plan out your day from the beginning to the end and abide by your time limits. Meetings and appointments will only run over if you allow them to. You will find that when you put hard stops on activities that they will magically adjust to fit the time allotted.

    I was sitting next to Mrs. Xernona Clayton, founder and CEO of The Trumpet Awards some years back at a function for the NAACP, where I had to introduce her on program. As soon as the program starts, she whispers over to me and says "I love when programs start on time. I'm never late to anything." I responded and said "Really. Never – to anything?". She repeats "Anything". I will never forget that moment because I learned a prime lesson about the importance of being on time for yourself and others. Hold yourself and others to being on-time. Lateness is another expectation that you are setting with others. If it becomes acceptable to arrive 1-5 minutes later, then it will become the norm.

    Time is of the essence. We've heard it before. Especially, if you are in freelance work or if you work a 9-5 job. Your professional time can be measured and should be measured. Put it in terms of the money you'll make. If someone is paying you, the rate they're willing to pay is the value. For example, if you spend 10 hours working each day, you get paid for those hours.

    If you run a business on the side that you eventually want to bring you into full-time work so you can quit your 9-5, that time's value is the eventual hourly rate. Of course, you have to take into account the extra hours you needed to make that money or seal the deal. If you're a consultant looking for a contract or a publicist looking for a client, you spend time looking for that contract and lining up your prospective clientele. If you spend four days to land a six-week gig that pays 500 dollars, you're making $500 for six weeks and four days, which is $14/day. That is not enough to live off of, so that means you need to raise your rates.

    You can spend a decent amount of time in your 3 checks of emails per day on emails if you find that the majority of your deal closings are via email and the same comparative nature applies to being on the phone. If it brings business, it makes perfect sense for you to spend two hours a day doing email because you received a $2,500 contract via email. But, if you check email two hours each day, that's 25% of your work hours if you are working 8 hour days. If you get paid $80,000 a year, then that email time has to bring in at least 25% of that $80,000 or $20,000 in order to be paying for itself.

If you want to flip money, increasing your cash flow, maximizing your time – all ultimate goals of thriving entrepreneurs – you have to do the math and figure out how much time you need to put into specific areas. When valuing income-producing time, divide the income by the total amount of time – billable and not – that it took to get that business.

There is a professional time that you can flip into money and then there is personal time that you can flip into money. If you missed something personal, how much would you charge yourself?   Let's take this example – your friend is getting married and you are a groomsman or a bridesmaid. But, you have been offered an extra shift at work. You have already decided that you are going to go to the wedding anyway even though you would be paid overtime on your job. Of course, it is a risk that you are taking reasonably and morally based on understandable judgement. But how much are you charging yourself to take advantage of your personal time?

Set your rate per hour, not just for others but for yourself. What would you charge to miss something personal? Whatever that number is, that is the value you're placing on that particular personal time.

Personal time can be spent on personal development which externally reveals itself, gleaning off of people who have strong character. It creates opportunity for exposure. A major modern currency is "exposure". Is it worth your time to work for "exposure"? If it has indirect but deliberate financial lead, it may very well be worth your time. Convert the payoff to dollars. When you're offered access or exposure instead of money, ask how much you would be willing to pay for the equivalent access. Let's say you're a motivational speaker who is just getting out there and waiting to get introduced to a large scaled speaker circuit and you are offered the chance to speak in front of an audience of 15,000 but it would be an unpaid gig. Is it a good deal? Should you take it?

Ask yourself: if they had not offered, how much would you be willing to pay to be on that stage? Just asking that question immediately puts you in a new frame of mind. You start being picky. You ask how many people will be there and streaming live. You think of the number of impressions, reach and engagement. Will you be on the flyer with fellow guest speakers that inspire you? How will they promote the appearance? How much will it raise (or lower) your credibility to speak? The simple act of asking what you would pay leads you immediately to ask a bunch of questions that you might not think to ask otherwise.

It all goes back to the question: Is it worth my time? Does everything align to make reasonable, good sense. When figuring out what you'd pay for exposure, make sure to consider its effect on your reputation. In the modern era of internet exploitation vs, the 80s/90s era of tabloid exploitation, you have to always think of your personal brand. What does it look like now and what type of legacy in your industry, career, and family do you want to leave?

There is a reason why a famous entertainer or public figure would charge $75,000 to attend a gathering: their reputation gives the gathering higher status. On the other hand, however, if you are not famous or reach notoriety, accepting free exposure can damage your brand. Accepting less than what you're worth sets a precedent, so factor the reputation effects into how you value exposure.

Now, you've converted all your options into dollar mounts, but you are still not finished yet because each option is not equally likely. That event you were offered to speak at unpaid will feature 15,000 in attendance. What if you are placed during an odd time in the program or given an unequal amount of time compared to other speakers? Let's say the other speakers are getting paid $2,500. You estimate the chance of remaining consistently engaged with 10% of that crowd, be it 1,500, which might still be great on a high end. Multiply the dollar value, $2,500, by the probability of 10%, you get $250 as the value of the time you would spend speaking at that event. That's your expected value.

Of course, there are numbers and then there is just your guts. When numbers fail, there's always an old standby. There are subconscious factors that you that you want to take into consideration like whether or not you will be miserable doing the high value gig or happy doing the low value gig. If your gut gives a different answer than you brain, then somewhere along the lines, you overlooked something. You gave time the wrong value or overlooked important pieces of currency. Go back and re-value your time, but correct your valuation based on the feedback from your gut.

Valuing our time is about making tradeoffs because there is only so much time in a day. You simply cannot get every single thing done and not everything can take up your attention. It does not work that way. You have to choose what is most important versus what can be put off to the side. For personal time, ask what you would have to be paid to give up that time. For exposure, ask what you would be willing to pay for the equivalent exposure. Then multiply by the probability that you will really get that payoff and you have your dollar mount. Then always double-check with your gut to make sure that everything lines up. Yes, time may be about money, but it is up to you to decide how much money that is. You know what it takes for you to feel comfortable or reach the level of financial success that you are looking for.

One of the biggest mistakes we make in life is having a poor use of our time. Jobs and commitments have a tendency of overwhelming us because the free time that we have outside of these jobs and commitments are misused and that plays a huge role in our sense of fulfillment.

You can either live life in the past, present, or future. Some choose to linger around try to fill the void of time with whatever entertains them at the moment. Others create goals that are in hopes of getting more pleasure. Then there are those who choose to find something they enjoy and spend as much time as they can on it. Live life on purpose. Spend your time on purpose. Everything you do must revolve around purpose.

Create goals with purpose and a sense of fulfillment so that it is not just another solution to a problem but a lead to fulfillment and happiness.

The more time we give to others, the more often we find ourselves in situations where our value fades away and we lose touch with our sense of fulfillment, growth and adventure.

When you are younger, you think you know what makes you happy until other things come along that make you happy. Then when time goes by and something across to rob you of your happiness, we tend to get lost along our journey of discovery towards happiness. We eventually realize that there is no answer to what makes us happy. There is no amount of money or fame that gets us there. But the more time we spend on creating leads towards fulfilment and pleasure, happiness will come.

Sure, this can come from free time as long as it is constructive. Even vacations can be constructive. Free time must consist of activities that do not just merely eliminate boredom, but they are helping us become better, giving us new experiences, expanding our knowledge and improving our lives in new emotionally fulfilling and purposeful ways.

Live on purpose. This is not about doing something just because someone else is doing it or tells you to do it or informs you that you have been called or destined to do it. It is about what you choose to innately do for yourself that brings you purpose and fulfillment. God gives us this opportunity to empower our purpose by valuing our time in order that we may in-turn contribute to the world by being who we are and living with purpose.

I love to travel and meet new people, look over new horizons and gain new experiences. The more I grow, the more I can help others grow. I can contribute to the world by being who I am to the fullest and live with purpose.

Be careful what you choose to do with your time, even with good intentions. Sometimes the best intentions do not always bring the best outcomes.

If you are giving a lot and receiving little in return in terms of your own happiness and you feel it wouldn't be returned had the situation been reversed, that is a clear sign that you need to reevaluate how you're spending your time and who you are spending it with. I used to spend a lot of time around people who meant well and had good character but no motivation, no goals. It would be years before I see one inch of growth to come out of them. This was a detriment to my growth.

    Just because you choose to spend your time doing what gives you a sense of fulfillment it doesn't mean you care any less about your relationships, but it does mean that you are valuing your time most importantly and making it a priority. The point I am trying to make is who you choose to spend your time around will determine how you spend your time, so choose those who have similar goals, purposes and interests that bring fulfilment into your life.

    It takes time to build muscle because you need to have a good exercise routine, eat healthy and get plenty of rest.

    The same is true about conditioning your own sense of fulfillment.

    Take your time and grow a little more each week.

    Don't overdo it too soon.

    It's not about changing everything on day one. It's about steady growth. If it takes a year to replace bad habits and time-wasting activities, that's fine.

    The more time you spend doing what you love, the less time you will spend avoiding what you hate. By eliminating activities that suck up time and give little to nothing in return you increase your level of energy and your ability to handle tasks better.

    Focus on the few things that really matter to you and slowly eliminate the rest. Increasing your level of fulfillment is a practice.

You can't make being happy a goal that you will reach one day because goals have completion dates and once you meet that goal you have to fill it with something new or you'll revert back to feeling depressed and unfulfilled. Instead choose to practice doing the things you love more and more while also practicing to spend less time on the things that bore you or cause you to waste your time.

Increasing your level of fulfillment is just as much about getting rid of pointless activities as it is filling your time with things you enjoy. If you take your time, build yourself up and condition yourself for the mental and physical changes that you desire you'll get there.

Start out spending 10 to 15 min a day doing something you enjoy, make it a habit and slowly and steadily increase your time on that one activity till you've built that desire up. Once you have that down and it becomes instinctive, start focusing on another activity you enjoy and repeat the process. The point is to slowly filter out the activities that waste your time and give you nothing in return.

Over the course of a year you can take baby steps that will allow you to recreate yourself and help you to condition a better you. Believe me, a lot can change in a year. Conditioning a better life comes from trying different things and figuring out what you truly enjoy and what you thought you would but you don't.

If you find fulfillment in what you do than continue doing it, but if you don't you may want to experiment with new activities until you find something that increases your sense of fulfillment. Don't simply give yourself goals and activities because you want to avoid boredom, choose things that you believe will help you to feel more fulfilled. The best activities are those that help you grow and can bring you fulfillment years after you start them.

If you love playing sports and you'll feel the same way 5 years later than you've found something really worth pursuing.

So, why do you need to value your time? Just so people will respect you? Absolutely not, there is nothing to do with respect from other people in this. It is all about you, valuing your own time. It's about not letting someone tell you they are going to underpay you and you letting them. If you're a writer, an artist, or literally anyone, value yourself and value the time you have.

Life is short, but it also is your forever.

If someone offers you twenty dollars for six hours of work, tell them **no**. You are worth more than that. Value yourself. You are worth being paid enough to live on. You are worth the "Thank you," for going out of your way to help someone else. It is worth it to make as much of your time as you absolutely can.

How do you value your time? Where do you start? How can you make the most of it? These are questions I asked myself too. As a freelancer, I have let people walk all over me because I need money and appreciated opportunities. But, eventually there came a time when I decided that enough is enough.

KEY #3 - BE TRANSPARENT

The Key To Transparency and Mentorship

What does transparency mean? Transparency means openness and honesty. Transparency is intentionally baring your soul to the world to show your true self to others. Most people hide their essence in fear of rejection, lack of self-confidence, broken-hearted, or lack of fulfillment in life. These are just a few of the many reasons why people hold back who they are. When a person hides behind this veil, they are robbing themselves of a happy and contented life.

To their surprise, they don't often realize people actually would prefer to know the "real" them. Through transparency, people are allowing themselves to feel their emotions without trying to understand or "fix" them. This is a way to give yourself permission to feel and experience your feelings rather than reflect on them. The creation from this process is a power that comes from within. It is a peace and freedom of one's self.

I read that transparency reveals the character of a person and I could not agree more. Feelings of fear, rejections, low self-esteem, and broken hearts (to name a few) create uneasiness within us and this leads to internal negative thoughts or thoughts. These thoughts can drown out our essence; the same place transparency grows from.

Transparency removes feelings of uneasiness and drowns out the negative internal voices; this process builds power from within and helps to create positive living.

I want you to note the things that prevent you from living a transparent life.

Then, ask yourselves the following questions:

-What actions can you implement to become more transparent?
-What benefits do you think you would obtain by living transparently?
-What risks are you willing to take to live transparently?

If you own a business or in a position of freelance in any capacity, transparency has to be at the core of your character. The biggest reason why is that you need people and people need you. A business cannot exist without customers. Artists cannot top the charts without fans. Actors cannot release blockbusters without people going to the movies and impressing the box office. You need people and people need you. So, your life has to become a social campaign to garner people with your specific, unique messaging. It is a matter of informing more and more people of your character and helping them envision their placement in your journey of growth to getting where God wants you to be. Transparency is at the core of it because you do not just want acquisition but you want brand loyalty. Do people know the real you?

It starts with honesty. Honesty is the doorway to transparency.

Webster defines honesty this way: "Fairness and straightforwardness of conduct and adherence to fact." Other dictionaries define honesty as "speaking truth in all varieties of communication, both verbal and non-verbal, being without deception." But this is the definition I have found the most useful: "Honesty means consistent loyalty to truth."

Here's the reason I've found this definition so useful: Loyalty means faithfulness without question. In other words, what you are loyal to… you follow without question. The word "loyalty" is important here, because it's the act of binding yourself (intellectually or emotionally) to a course of action. So, when you're loyal to truth, it suggests there is no conflict of interest within your own mind. Your loyalty is to truth, and that is without question.

Why does loyalty to truth = honesty?

When it comes to communicating our intentions and motives, things can get pretty complicated. But the fact remains that every choice, every action, and every word that comes out of our mouth bears witness to what values we are loyal to.

You can easily verify this yourself, to see if this is true for you.

Observe for a day other people's conversations, and you'll soon have clues about what values they are secretly loyal to. At the end of the day, what is done in the dark comes to the light. The way they communicate lets you know if they're loyal to being right or wrong, loyal to winning or losing, loyal to fitting in or standing out, or loyal to making a good impression or being present.

Honest people are loyal to truth above all other values. This means they don't lie to avoid hurting feelings; they don't misrepresent to make a favorable impression; and they won't manipulate or use deceptive tactics to gain unfair advantages.

So how loyal to the truth are you really?

Your loyalty to truth can be measured in your consistency. The word "consistent" is important here, because the more consistently loyal to truth you are, the more of an honest a person you are. Notice, I said consistently loyal (not perfectly loyal); that's because honesty isn't about perfection, it's about consistency. The opposite is also true. Inconsistency suggests a willingness to abandon truth because it might help you gain benefits or avoid negative consequences. The more inconsistent you are in your loyalty to truth, the more dishonest you become.

But why is honesty (loyalty to truth) so important when it comes to inspiring transparency? It all comes down to one word: Trust. Those who are loyal to truth inspire trust. And that trust is what makes it safe for others to be transparent with you.

Transparency is important to build relationships with anyone: a significant other, a mentor, a colleague, a friend. Just as there can be no trust without honesty, there's no real intimacy without transparency because they do not know the real you.

And what is a relationship of any kind without intimacy or trust? That's right, not much.

This falls into the compliance of trends. Dysfunction Is created by dishonest actions. Dishonesty is the opposite of honesty. However, that definition is so simple that many fail to understand the full range of dishonesty. Because not only is dishonesty the absence of honesty, it's also the denial of truth and the defaulting on your responsibility to be honest.

The truth about dishonesty: Dishonesty includes excuses and rational lies used to default on meeting our responsibilities. Being in denial means being dishonest with yourself about a truth or fact. Wishing things were different is a form of denial (dishonesty) because the reality is that, things are the way they are (truth).

Dishonesty is misrepresenting our true feelings to avoid hurting others.

If dishonesty were an icing cake, it would be available in two flavors: emotional dishonesty and verbal dishonesty.

Some examples of verbal dishonesty: Lying (including little white lies), Exaggerations (overstating the truth), Misdirection (omission, manipulation, and withholding), Excuses (indirectness, vagueness, and avoidance), Pretense (faking it)

Some examples of emotional dishonesty: Denial (pretending to want what you don't want, hiding what you do want), Projection (attacking, accusing, blaming, and condemning to cover your own fears and anger), Misrepresenting intentions, motives, desires, and emotions, Rationalizations and excuses (using the intellect to buffer against facing consequences)

The thing to note is that any form of dishonesty leads to dysfunction in a relationship. And a dysfunctional relationship is just not healthy enough (or safe enough) for transparency to flourish. So, if you want to inspire transparency, begin by eliminating all types of dysfunctional habits — especially dishonesty.

If you want to build strong, meaningful relationships, make it safe for other people to be honest with you. It starts by removing these three perpetrators:

- Remove the fear of hurting each other's feelings. This is a classic excuse for relationship dishonesty. In an attempt to avoid hurt feelings, couples tell each other what they want to hear, rather than being honest about how they feel. The way to remove this culprit is for both being in the relationship to take responsibility for their own feelings.
- Remove the fear of punishment. Adults are deceptive for the same reason children are deceptive: because they fear the truth will get them into trouble. One way to remove this culprit is to reward truth rather than punish lies. This is far more effective because people are more likely to do what brings rewards.
- Remove the inhibitions and perceived lack of safety. The reality is that people will only be as honest as they feel safe to be. If you're the type of person who's quick to judge, easily offended, or highly sensitive, then the person you are in the relationship with might feel inhibited in being honest. If this is the case, then you've got to make it safe for others to tell you the truth before you can expect them to do so.

What you hide is what you keep because what is done in the dark comes to the light. The parts of ourselves we hide are the parts we don't like — the parts that we feel ashamed of or are guilty about — and that's why we lock them away in the basement of our lives. But just because we hide something doesn't mean it's gone. Living transparently means airing out the closets and sweeping out the cobwebs from under the bed. It means to come out of hiding… to walk in the light… to learn how to be OK with your flaws, faults, and shortcomings.

This takes bravery at its best. And when you do this, it allows you to have compassion for others. This is the key to it all because the goal of living transparently is to learn how to live honestly. Once you're truly being honest, then you honestly have to admit that you're not the exception. True, we are special, but not really because in another sense we are all the same. We are all prime examples of what it means to be humans.

This is both a humbling and an exhilarating thought because it means you belong to the same group as Nelson Mandela and Martin Luther King Jr. As you think about this, it suddenly becomes clear that none of them could have accomplished what they did by hiding themselves.

What about privacy? There's a difference between privacy and living transparently. Transparency is all about not hiding. This means not keeping secrets, not doing things in the dark that you wouldn't do in the light, and not saying things behind your partner's back that you wouldn't say to his or her face. On the other hand, privacy is a matter of boundaries.

Here's what I mean:

If your conversations, actions, and words are of a nature that you wouldn't be comfortable saying or doing them when your partner is present, or if you engage in actions or activities that you feel you have to protect or hide, this means you're not living transparently.

If you have healthy boundaries in your relationship, then you allow each other the freedom to experience moments of privacy, solitude, introspection, and activities that are transparent but private (meaning your partner knows and respects your private time).

Be authentic. The word "authentic" comes from the Greeks, meaning "one who acts on his own authority." Not only is being authentic a state of awareness, it's also a way of being. The opposite of being authentic is of course being inauthentic.

Classic examples of being inauthentic include:

-Selling out (the choice for approval above truth)
-Playing mind games
-Faking it (made-up reactions and responses)
-Saving face (the choice to impress rather than reveal ignorance)
-Using deceptive strategies to gain unfair advantages
-Doing whatever it takes to win, regardless of the consequences to self-esteem
-Living passively rather than creatively
-Defaulting on your responsibilities and commitments
-Living your life by default rather than by design
-Why is being true to yourself an important part of transparency?

Here's the beautiful truth:

You can't fake self-esteem. You can't fake happiness. The two require authenticity. They have to be real to be valid. If you ever want to feel comfortable in your own skin, to quit seeking external approval, to stop apologizing for who you are, to stop playing small, to feel truly connected to your partner, to embrace true love and to enjoy transparency as a part of your everyday experience, then being authentic is the path that takes you home to yourself. If you want to be trustworthy, then it all begins with being true to yourself.

Being transparent is a powerful thing, if you can trust yourself and be trusted by others. The reason most leaders are not transparent is because they believe they will be viewed as less authoritative; that the credentials they worked so hard to attain will lose their power, leverage and gravitas. This is the problem with most leaders, they are not aware of the reality that exists around them. People want to relate to its leaders. People want to know that their leaders have experienced the same problems and/or how they have overcome personal hardships. The digital age has allowed people to learn more about their leaders. As such, social media has suddenly given people the permission to enter a leader's personal space; a place they were previously prohibited from entering. The digital age has changed the levels of transparency that we expect from people too.

We are all living during a time when people want and expect their leaders to be more human, less perfect and at times a bit vulnerable – regardless of hierarchy or rank. This need for transparency in society is at an all-time high. There is a reason people would rather "see" a video blog than "read" a blog. They want access to one's facial expressions, eye contact and body language. People want to evaluate whether someone is acting or being genuine.

Embracing transparency requires more than mere words. It requires work, effort, courage, and commitment. Living transparently is worth it.

The fact of the matter is that the journey of transparency is quite difficult to navigate on one's own. This is why you need a mentor.

What can a mentor do for you? Your mentor will have a lot of wisdom to share. Mentors can help you understand and react in more productive ways to complicated or unusual situations, or at the very least offer a new perspective on what might be a difficult issue. Mentors can help you feel more confident in your decisions, direct you to better resources, advise you on what skills you might lack, and provide some depth on long-standing education topics.

Mentors can introduce you to other administrative professionals and leaders, helping you expand your professional community. Your mentor becomes someone you value.

No matter who you are and how accomplished you have become, you need a mentor. You need someone who can provide direction, pick you up when you fall, dust you off, and send you back out. The cost of missing out on mentorship is high. An HR study found that employees who received mentoring were promoted five times more often than people who didn't have mentors. It has also been estimated that startups with helpful mentors are seven times more likely to raise investment money.

How can you land a great mentor? You can start by avoiding these seven mentorship sins, some of which you may already be committing, and you'll be well on your way.

1. Asking for the Mentor Upfront

If you met a girl you like, would you ask her to marry you on the first date. Probably not. Well, if you do, it'd be a terrible idea. Being so abrupt is a bad idea on a first date, and you should treat your first encounter with a mentor the same way. There isn't enough time or information in one meeting to predict if a mentorship bond exists between you. Your best bet is to ask for the meeting; not the mentorship. Most people will grant you a 15-minute conversation to answer any specific questions. Here's a line that always works: "I enjoyed our conversation. Should a specific question arise, would it be okay if I reached out for a 15-minute chat to continue the conversation?"

2. Not Establishing Rules for Following Up

You get one chance to make an impression on a potential mentor. Use this time to set up an agreement for your next encounter. The goal is to set rules of engagement. But usually, when you set expectations upfront, if you send a message, they will refer back to the email chain and honor the request.

3. Asking Questions You Can Easily Google

Engage your mentor with a cloud of questions that are they are qualified to answer, but also bring quality to the conversation.

4. Making It All About You

The idea that some mentor will imbue a young Mark Zuckerberg or Oprah Winfrey with all the knowledge he or she needs to succeed is untrue. Quite frankly, it's inconsiderate to all of the other people who do not have that kind of access. The truth is, in today's noisy competition for mentors, two-way relationships are the most likely to succeed. Mentors appreciate the value that is added to their lives from their mentees. Whether it be them volunteering at events, playing the role of a confidant every once in a while, or simply traveling to support them.

7. Not Expressing Gratitude

Never underestimate the power of gratitude in a mentor relationship. Updated emails tracking your progress and expressing genuine appreciation for your mentors' help goes a long way.

Decide why you want a mentor. Whether you're looking for someone with a similar skill set to guide you through a career path or hoping to learn new skills, pinpoint what you're looking for.

Find a mentor. Networking is a great way to find a good match. Attend industry events, join professional groups and associations, and consider former colleagues.

Create goals for your mentoring relationship. Tighten the focus by writing a list of objectives, such as strengthening your interviewing skills or polishing your resume. Discuss them with your mentor at the start of your relationship, and review them regularly to make sure you're on course and the relationship is working.

Determine how you'll stay in touch. While you might prefer weekly check-ins via email, your mentor might request monthly phone chats. Talk with your mentor to decide how often you'll communicate, and whether it's by phone, Skype, email, or chat. Regular communication is key to establishing a bond and getting great results. Meeting face to face, especially in the beginning, can help establish a deeper connection, so be sure to schedule a few in-person meetings.

Build trust. After you earn your mentor's trust, he or she will share more with you. Act responsibly to gain it. Never cancel appointments. Follow up on leads in a timely and professional manner.

Soak up knowledge. Always be attentive when your mentor shares advice and skills. Be an active listener and proactive in applying what you've learned. Ask for feedback and graciously accept his or her corrections — don't get defensive.

Be thankful. Becoming a mentor is a big responsibility that takes a lot of time, so always treat your mentor with respect, courtesy and appreciation. Don't demand too much of your mentor's time or request too many favors or introductions to contacts. Work around your mentor's schedule and be patient when a request isn't answered immediately. Mentors tend to give a lot in the relationship, so recognize that by thanking your mentor regularly.

Mix it up. There are many ways to learn from your mentor. To get the most out of the relationship, vary the types of things you do together. For example, ask your mentor about his or her past experiences, review written materials like your resume and cover letter, and discuss your goals, plan of action, and skill development. Invite your mentor to attend professional events like conferences and meetings. You can also ask your mentor if it's possible to shadow him or her at work.

Meet more mentors. Don't feel that you need to limit yourself to one mentor. People have different experiences and skill sets. By building relationships with other individuals in your field, you'll be expanding your network and your knowledge base.

Your Network is Your Net Worth

You invest in your money, but do you invest in your relationships? I know way too many people who spend an outrageous amount of time on researching the perfect life with their favorite cars and houses, ideal bank account balance, and credit lines. I was spending too much time focusing on the value of the wrong set of assets.

I believe your social capital, or your ability to build a network of authentic personal and professional relationships, not your financial capital, is the most important asset in your portfolio. I believe that seeking out and working in collaboration with others who share your interests and values will provide a stronger foundation, enabling you to reach a higher level of success than you would on your own. Therefore, I believe that your "net worth" will be based not on the size of your portfolio or the size of your network but on your ability to define and stay true to your passions and values and that working with other people who share them will allow you to build a strong and enduring interpersonal safety net that will carry you through any financial calamity to greater output and personal fulfillment.

One reason your network is your net worth is that how we work, along with the role of the employer, has been completely transformed. Globalization, changes in digital technology, and a wavering economy have made tens of millions of corporate positions more contingent and less secure. The reality is that no matter how much you like your job or your company, you can, at any given time, be forced into unemployment. With few workplaces guarantees, it's important to recognize your best path to job security is yourself. The more adaptive, flexible, and agile you are, the more you'll succeed. Look internally, not externally, for happiness and job security. Build your skill sets, improve your network, ask questions, and don't assume that others will take charge of your career.

Your network is also your net worth because we've entered a new era where shifting cultural values and improved technology enable us to network in vastly improved, more focused, and more enjoyable ways that are more in tune with our personalities and passions. Technology has accelerated networking, reduced the degree of separation between contacts, amplified our global playing field, and redefined the job prospecting process. It's easier to find niche communities' online, new relationships may be just a tweet away and existing relationships may hold more value than you realize.

Your network is also your net worth, because at the end of the day, what is life really about: head, heart or wallet?

Whether you goal is to focus on your head, your heart or your wallet; remember, building and strengthening your network will help you improve your happiness, productivity, and true net worth. I encourage you to focus on your passions, surround yourself with people that share your values and don't let your social capital lie dormant. Reinvest it! And remember, *your network is your net worth.*

A strong network is like money in the bank. Your network can help you build visibility, connect you with influencers, and open up doors for new opportunities. Building and nurturing a network is one of the most powerful things you can do to support your career advancement. Yet often, our networking efforts are just social, haphazard, and as a result, ineffective. You make friends and connections; however, these people are not always in a position to help you further your career or most importantly, they may not be willing to speak for you.

Here are 5 ways to build social capital:

1. **Network proactively.**
Networking proactively is important. What happens if you don't have a strong network, and suddenly you lose your job? If you don't have a network to tap into, you're out of luck. It will most likely take you much longer to find a new position. And how can you get information about a hiring manager or new boss if you don't have a network of people to provide that information?

Networking proactively provides an advantage by supporting you with a powerful collection of people who are willing and able to speak for you on an ongoing basis. The network is there for you when you need it because you've built the social capital.

2. **Be strategic.**
Strategic networking is more than socializing and swapping business cards, it's creating solid relationships to support your career aspirations. It takes focus and intention to build such a network, but it's invaluable for your professional development.

Identify who you know and who you need to know to help you reach your career goal and build a power network to support your advancement.

3. **Create a diverse network.**
In order to network effectively, you need to move out of your comfort zone and identify people who can help your career, not just those people you like.

Highly open networks, a diverse set of individuals who don't know one another, is often associated with faster promotions, higher bonuses, and strong performance reviews.

4. **Pay it forward and leverage relationships.**
Truly effective networking—networking in the manner of the high earning and high career-level elite professionals represented within this study—requires more than 'connections' or 'friends'; it requires cutting through clutter and focusing on what matters—real, mutually beneficial partnerships."

Identifying the right people, those people who have power and influence and who are willing to recommend you, is the first step. Building and nurturing relationships of trust is next. The third important step is to leverage the relationships by paying it forward, being willing to help others and asking for assistance when you need it.

5. **Set aside dedicated time each week to network.**
One of the major push backs I hear from women is they don't have time to network. They scramble to get their job done during the day and at night they often have family responsibilities that prevent them from networking activities.

If you don't schedule time each week, your default behavior will be to stay in your office and tackle your to do list. Schedule at least one networking meeting per week. Make it your intention to have lunch or coffee with colleagues and key stakeholders. Put it on your calendar or it won't happen!

Your time is valuable so be strategic about your networking activity outside of work. It's wise to identify a couple of organizations that will provide valuable resources for your professional development. Before you join, go to a couple of meetings. Find those organizations that align with your values and offer you the best opportunities to build powerful relationships.

6. **Keep in touch with former colleagues and alums.**
While it's important to build a network of contacts to support your career goal, it's equally important to nurture the relationships you have. Former colleagues, bosses, alums already know the value you offer and can recommend you for new opportunities. It pays to stay in touch. I know from my

own experience how important these relationships are. And I have heard countless stories of other women have turned to their network for support for new business ventures, promotions, and connections to influencers.

7. Focus your social media networking efforts.

One would think that because we are constantly connected online, that networking in this manner is easy. After all, we have the potential for tremendous exposure to a vast network of people. However, online professional networking is not without challenges.

It is difficult to cut through all the noise. The number of people who connect with us is daunting and as a result, it's easy to lose our strategic focus. Someone approaches us on Facebook, Twitter, or LinkedIn, or any other social network and asks to connect and our first response is to say ok. We end up with a huge network of people we don't know and who offer us no value. It's wiser to look carefully at their profiles to determine if you want that person in your network. If you determine there is some commonality, then reply and set up some time to talk and initiate a relationship. The point is that the number of contacts in your online network is not nearly as important as the quality.

We are frequently told about the importance of networking. Yet we are not necessarily taught how to network in a strategic manner to support our career aspirations. The best way to move your career ahead is to build and nurture mutually beneficial relationships with people who can speak for you and create the visibility you need to succeed.

With today's immense competition and the growing global market, this phrase is truer than ever. Lucky for us, technology has made networking a piece of cake. Even so, the art of network building and maintenance remains a mystery to many.

Throughout the years, I've witnessed individuals obtain life-changing opportunities because of their connections.

Clear Communication Requires Clear Thinking

Clear thinking is the ability to express ideas in a simple and straightforward manner. It also involves the ability to analyze statements and follow logical arguments. Some people imagine it means being super-clever or having a high IQ. Others think it's the ability to solve really difficult puzzles or unravel complex statements. But in fact, it's none of these things.

Clear thinking means that you have the ability to express your own ideas simple and think in a logical manner. I would rather be a clear thinker than an analytic thinker. I would take both if I had that opportunity but I would choose one out of the two, I would choose clear thinking.

Here is the deal – if you are in business, education, and all forms of intellectual life, clear thinking is a vital part of effective communication. It's what's called a 'core skill' which will enable you to think, speak, and write in an effective manner.

If you want to persuade people, develop powerful arguments or become more discerning and precise you need to have clear thinking.

Communicating the results of clear thinking becomes easier for the writer who starts with a logical, organized argument supported by the facts. There is a natural, persuasive flow to this argument and, consequently, a reader is more likely to understand and be convinced by what is written.

Clear writing founded on clear thinking will be direct, organized, and concise. It will avoid stridency or complexity; it will be free of jargon and inflated language; it will favor concreteness over abstraction. Clear writers write to express, not impress.

Yet the clear writer does not have to sacrifice aesthetics in pursuit of clarity: active verbs, varied sentence lengths, vivid descriptions, and precise language are all part of clear writing and can be shaped into a distinctive, appealing style. Clear writing, like clean design in architecture, can offer both functionality and grace.

Clear thinking is a search for precision, clarity, and truthfulness. You can develop the skills required by breaking down what you say and write into small and simple units. Simplicity usually leads to greater clarity. You also need to analyze arguments and recognize their underlying logic.

You need to take into consideration mental effort and discipline. Pay very close attention to the small details of what you say, read, and write. If expressed in a clear and logical manner than the claims that you make are pretty powerful. Substantiate evidence and facts to support them. The claims other people make should be inspected very closely and examined for their truthfulness, their logic, and their validity as arguments.

Do not over simplify things and overcomplicate things by using confusing language.

If communication is defined as a meaningful exchange of information, thoughts and feelings between two living creatures, critical thinking is the engine that provides this meaning. Communication starts with a thought, a feeling and an emotion. The mind builds on this thought before putting it out to the receiver. Critical thinking, quite simply, is the tool to coherently build our thoughts. Effective communication starts with a clear thought process. Critical thinking breeds clarity of thought.

A constant pursuit of critical thinking equips leaders and managers think rationally, provide sound reasoning and develop a coherent argument. When leaders think critically and communicate clearly, they are also able to eliminate ambiguity in communication.

Communication is as much about listening as it is about delivering. Listening involves a careful interpretation of what is being said, not said, the meaning behind it and the intent. It requires a leader to consider arguments from others, elicit alternative perspectives and distill facts. Critical thinking allows a leader to exercise restraint while listening and helps in following the thought process of the other party. Critical thinking helps a leader in responding effectively in a given context rather than reacting.

'Listening to the self' is also an important part of communication process. Critical thinkers possess higher awareness of their own beliefs, experiences and biases. Critical thinking enables them to think beyond the barriers of their own biases.

Critical thinking builds confidence in communication. It is far easier to communicate when you are prepared with facts, arguments, perspectives and possible solutions.

Communicating is one thing. Communicating in a way that delivers maximum impact is another. Critical thinking is a tool to structure your key messages in a way that delivers maximum impact.

Critical thinking and communication are intricately connected. Effective communication requires clarity of thought, ability to listen intentionally and deliver messages in the most optimal way.

Organizations can address a lot of their communication problems if they are careful about evaluating critical thinking skills when hiring the leaders and developing a culture of critical thinking. Improving how people think is a great way to start improving the quality of overall communication in the organization. Once people think clearly, rationally and critically, external communication training interventions will also yield desired results.

Critical thinking is the driver of effective communication.

Make People Feel Important & Empower Others

Investors invest in people, not ideas. Customers buy from people, not companies. Employees rally for a great leader. As an entrepreneur, you need relationships to succeed. That means relationships with team members, investors, customers, and vendors. One of the best ways to build a good relationship with anyone is to make them feel important.

I have always told authors that people fall in love with the author before they fall in love with the book. Entrepreneurs: people connect with that entrepreneurial spirit before they solely connect with the idea. You have a

There is a book by Brian Tracy, called "No Excuses! The Power of Self-Discipline" and in it he outlines seven ways to make other people feel important, which I believe are extremely relevant to entrepreneurs and business:

1) Accept people the way they are. Because most people are judgmental and critical, to be unconditionally accepted by another person raises that person's self-esteem, reinforces his or

her self-image, and makes that person much more likely to accept you and follow your lead.

2) Show your appreciation for others. When you appreciate another person for anything that he or she has done or said, they will like themselves and you more as well. The simplest way to express appreciation is to simply say, "Thank you" for an idea, some good feedback, time spent together, or an order.

3) Be agreeable. The most welcomed people in every situation are those who are generally agreeable and positive with others. Entrepreneurs who like to be argumentative, complaining, or disagreeable, will have a hard time closing a contract, investment, or a customer contract.

4) Show your admiration. People invest a lot of personal emotion in their possessions, traits, and accomplishments. When you admire something belonging to another person, it makes him feel happy about himself. Everyone has positives, and it's up to you to find them. In turn, these positives will be reflected back on you.

5) Pay attention to others. The most powerful way to pay attention to someone is to listen attentively first, even ask questions, before you launch into a monologue answering every question they might never ask. Believe it or not, before you even say a word, you will become a more interesting and intelligent person in their eyes.

6) Never criticize, condemn, or complain. In business as well as personal relationships, the most harmful force of all is destructive criticism. It lowers a person's self-esteem, makes him feel angry and defensive, and causes him to dislike you. If your target is someone not present, it still causes a loss of trust in you, since your listener could be the next target.

7) Be courteous, concerned, and considerate of everyone you meet. When you treat a person with courtesy and respect, they will value and respect you more. By being concerned, you

connect with their emotions. Consideration is the discipline to do and say things to people that are important to them.

Think back on your own recent experiences as a customer or contractor. You don't always buy the cheapest product or service, if you have a good relationship with the people involved. On the other hand, I almost never buy from someone that treats me like I'm not important.

If you want to be a leader, you need to inspire followership. Great leaders develop a good relationship with good people, who are then inspired to follow. A successful leader inspires people to do more than they might have done without the relationship, and more than they may have even dreamed possible.

So, if you follow all these seven ways to make other people feel important, you will receive a seven-fold payback on your own objectives of being a leader and building a successful business. That's a lot cheaper and lot longer lasting than the best advertising and public relations you can buy.

Do not talk so much. So many people think making other people feel comfortable and entertained is about saying the right things, but the real trick isn't talking well, it's listening well, and for that you need to actually shut your mouth.

Make other people feel like an expert. Pump them up. I do it all of the time. I want to make sure that when I meet new people and have expertise in a particular area that they know I respect their tenure in this endeavor.

Another thing you must do is focus on focusing. If you want the other person to feel like they're at the center of your world, unsurprisingly, it helps to actually put them at the center of your world for the duration of your conversation.

There are other ways to get distracted too, such as scanning the room for other people you want to meet, fiddling with your hair or hands, or letting other worries or concerns divide your attention. Eliminate those distractions too if you're aiming for killer charisma.

Mind your body language. It is everything! All of these tricks won't work if your questions say, 'I'm interested' but your body says 'I'm nervous and distracted,' so mind a few body language basics as well.

Empowering people is the key to building a high-performance team. Once you empower people by learning how to motivate and inspire them, they will want to work with you to help you achieve your goals in everything you do. Your ability to enlist the knowledge, energy and resources of others enables you to become a multiplication sign, to leverage yourself so that you accomplish far more than the average person and in a far shorter period of time.

Determine the Key People to Empower

There are three types of people that you want to and need to empower on a regular basis. They are, first of all, the people closest to you: your family, your friends, your spouse and your children. Second are your work relationships: your staff, your coworkers, your peers, your colleagues and even your boss. Third are all the other people that you interact with in your day-to-day life: your customers, your suppliers, your banker, the people with whom you deal in stores, restaurants, airplanes, hotels and everywhere else. In each case, your ability to get people to help you is what will make you a more powerful and effective person.

Always Be Positive

Empower means "putting power into," and it can also mean "bringing energy and enthusiasm out of." So, the first step in empowering people is to refrain from doing anything that disempowers them or reduces their energy and enthusiasm for what they are doing.

There are things you can do every single day to empower people and make them feel good about themselves.

Satisfy the Deepest Needs

The deepest need that each person has is for <u>self-esteem</u>, a sense of being important, valuable and worthwhile.

Everything that you do in your interactions with others affects their <u>self-esteem</u> in some way. You already have an excellent frame of reference to determine the things that you can do to boost the self-esteem and therefore the sense of personal power of those around you. Give them what you'd like for yourself.

Continually Express Appreciation

Perhaps the simplest way to make another person feel good about himself or herself is your continuous expressions of appreciation for everything that person does for you, large or small. Say "thank you" on every occasion.

Thank your spouse for everything that he or she does for you. Thank your children for their cooperation and support in everything that they do around the house. Thank your friends for the smallest acts of kindnesses. The more you thank other people for doing things for you, the more things those other people will want to do.

Valuing Relationships: Leads to Customers

First things first, everyone you meet and know is a lead. Your job is to, in some capacity, make them a customer. That does not have to mean that you are monetizing each person to make money off of them but you're retaining each person to devote towards brand loyalty.

Most of us probably know a fair amount of people on a variety of levels. Some are casual acquaintances that we know just because our paths cross on a regular basis. While we can't choose all of the people we encounter during the course of a normal day, there are certain people we choose to have in our lives. We call these people our friends.

Friendships also happens on a different level:

Let me ask you something:

1) How many real friendships do you have?
2) How many of those are really close friends?
3) Do you have a best friend?

There is an obvious point to those three questions. Do you see it?

The point is that friendships come in degrees. They're all important, but some are more important. A precious few are extremely important. I know it sounds obvious but many people fail to think this through logically. If there are only a precious few relationships that are "extremely" important in our life, what does that mean?

We need to prioritize those special friendships

Our actions and words need to send an unmistakable message to those people that they really do matter to us. One of the most common problems I see in relationships is that people just assume that their friend, mate, partner, or children somehow "know" how valued they are. They don't just know!

Meaningful friendships do not happen by accident, they need to be built and maintained. A close relationship also deserves our time and energy. If we take a relationship for granted, sooner or later it will fall apart. Where do you think the saying "I didn't know what I had until I lost it" came from?

Take a look at your closest friendships

Make sure that the way you treat those special people accurately expresses your true feelings. Make sure that your expressions are in harmony with your heart and that you are not sending mixed signals.

The most meaningful person in my life is my wife. We have been together through thick and thin for the last 27 years. She never has to wonder how I feel. She never needs to question my commitment to our marriage. She knows because I make certain that she knows. It's one of my highest priorities in life.

In your friendships choose quality over quantity

Sometimes it seems easier to put a man on the moon than to put a man and a woman under the same roof for any length of time. Why do you think that is? I'm sure the reasons vary, but no one ever made it to the moon without a giant commitment.

If you want to enjoy the benefits of a truly close and meaningful relationship, you must be willing to make a total commitment. I know that's a scary thought for many, but you simply can't have one without the other. In reality, a commitment is liberating. It says, I'm here no matter what. There is no exit strategy!

Adding value is what truly differentiates Real from other recruitment consultancies. Our sector and regional expertise brings recruitment insight to each and every relationship and means we can put the 'consult' back into recruitment consultancy.

Honesty, integrity and transparency are integral to what we do and how we ensure we collaborate at the highest levels, build relationships based on respect and understanding, and work with our partners to deliver success time after time.

Treating candidates and employers as equals ensures that none of our customers feel second best. This approach is critical for Real as we strive to build strong and long-lasting relationships with everyone we work with. It also means that every candidate and employer feels respected and valued, and that our commitment to partnering with one is not to the detriment of another.

Representing your best interests is what motivates Real to succeed. Whether you are a client or a candidate, your challenges and needs are what motivate us. They are what ensure the best and brightest talent continues to work with us exclusively; they are what make 60% of our business repeat business.

Never ignore a caring person. Firstly, never ignore a person who really cares for you. In this day and age, it really is quite hard to make time and prove to people that you really *do* care about them. Whoever that is trying to care for you is going out of their way to do so. Don't ignore them and don't hurt their feelings. This person is worth your time.

Make time. How many times have you heard, "Sorry, I can't come out sightseeing with you, *I've got no time*". The person that asks you to hang out with them has the time, so, why don't you? If your day is filled with activities that are really quite useless, get rid of them and make time for your partner. Try going for a walk to somewhere really beautiful with them. They'll appreciate it and so will you.

Help your children. Instead of just ignoring your children and letting them get on with life alone, help them up when they fall. Go into their rooms at nighttime, tuck them in and read them a bedtime story. Let them fall asleep to the sound of their mother's/father's voice. If they need help with their homework, talk them through it. don't just tell them to ask a sibling. They want *you* to help them. Also, let them tell you their silly gossip stories from school, it helps them build a close relationship with you.

Be a good friend. Everybody needs friends in their life. Friendships are one of the best kind of relationships. It can be hard to find a good, sincere friend these days but that doesn't mean that they're non-existent. When you do find a friend that is good to you, you *must* be good back to them to keep them as your friend. If you don't ever help them and just ignore them, they won't want to be your friend for much longer. Always be there for your friend when they need you and they'll surely return the favor.

Listen. Whether it's your mum, your dad, your teacher or your friend, to understand the importance of a relationship you must listen to their opinions and respect them. Without listening to them, you won't ever get to maintain a relationship long enough to fully understand how your relationship with them will affect your and their lives. Always keep your ears and your mind open to new ideas.

1. Personal Relationships

"Personal" means not just functional. You can have a functional relationship with someone because they are your doctor or lawyer or plumber or employer or pastor or teammate or teacher, without that relationship being personal. To be personal would mean that you would relate to each other about personal things, not just professional things.

Jesus had concentric circles of increasingly intimate personal relationships. There were the seventy that he appointed and sent out in Luke 10:1. Then there were the twelve that he chose to be with him throughout his entire ministry (Mark 3:14). Then there were Peter, James, and John. He took them with him onto the Mount of Transfiguration; into the house when he raised the little girl; and into the seclusion of the Garden of Gethsemane. He was personally closer to them than to the others. Finally, there was John who was called at least four times "the disciple whom Jesus loved." The point is that Jesus himself had a cluster of personal relationships in varying depths—and these did not become cliquish. Jesus had some deep personal relationships but he was open and outgoing to all.

One of the realities of a growing church is that neither the pastors nor anyone else can have personal relationships with everyone in the church. Our aim is not that everyone relates to everyone in a personal relationship, but that the atmosphere be so congenial to these kinds of relationships that they form easily and are prized and nurtured—that everyone has concentric circles of personal relationships the way Jesus did.

2. Deepening Relationships

The second word to describe the relationships we seek is "deepening." This simply means that we not stay at the level of superficiality—knowing a few personal things about people and asking glibly how things are going, but never going deeper with people.

3. Supportive Relationships

The third adjective we use to describe the relationships God is calling us to is "supportive." This is where love especially comes in. We are talking about relationships "of love." And love means that you have a heart to lighten people's load as you get to know them. Love means that your desire is to be a load-lifter, a burden-bearer, a helper, a strengthener.

It's true that we need all these things ourselves. But if you go into a relationship mainly to use the other person to meet your needs, it will very likely collapse. You will be most blessed if you live to be a blessing (Acts 20:35). Relationships thrive when we try to outdo each other in supporting not in being supported.

4. Faith-Building Relationships

Finally, we call these relationships of love "faith-building." Which means that the bottom line in why God designed us for relationships—which he did! —is so that we would help each other live by faith in future grace. Faith means "being satisfied with all that God is for us in Jesus." So, all Christian relationships have this as their goal: to help each other stay satisfied in God.

There are people right now in our church that are in a crisis of faith. Will they keep on trusting in God's future grace? I see all my preaching as a means of helping people stay satisfied in all that God is for us in Jesus. But preaching is not enough.

KEY #4 - BE HUMBLE

Accept Feedback and Assume Responsibility

Pushing yourself out of your comfort zone to take on more responsibility is a great way to grow personally and professionally. It can be uncomfortable and hard at times, but that's what will help you make real progress within an organization. So, give yourself a challenge, and try these five ways to step up and have your colleagues see you shine!

1. Talk to Your Boss

Go to your supervisor and see if there are any additional projects you can work on. Make it a discussion rather than a direct question: you can share your own career goals and talk about how you see yourself fitting into the company's future.

Think about what skills and knowledge you want to develop, and see if there's an opportunity that'll let you do just that. If possible, have a few concrete ideas in mind so you can suggest areas where you may be able to get more involved.

If you don't have regularly scheduled meetings with your supervisor, try to get time on his or her calendar for the conversation. But if that's a long way off, mention it in passing and follow up. A simple "Hey, I think I am ready for more responsibility and would like to help the team" may be just what he or she needs to know to give you the opportunity.

2. Look for Busy, Stressed Out Co-workers

Look for the people who need help, be it in other departments or in the cubicle next door, and offer to lend a hand. Make sure that you don't get taken advantage of, though, or become a victim of a credit hog: those colleagues who will attempt to have you do their extra work, and then take all the credit. Learn to identify and avoid these people.

Also, be sure <u>not to overwhelm yourself</u> with others' work. If you're risking neglecting your own responsibilities, you're going too far.

3. Become an Expert

Acquire new knowledge continuously and stay on top of trends or developments in your field. If you're seen as an expert in a particular subject, you're more likely to be needed for new projects coming up.

One simple way: set up a "Google Alert" for topics relevant to your industry, company, or team's area of responsibility. Pick your search terms, and any new articles featuring the terms you've chosen will be sent to your inbox in a daily update email. Another great option is to use <u>Twitter's news hashtags</u>.

When you find articles relevant to your team's work, send them out with a brief accompanying summary. You'll be helping all of your teammates look better and stay up-to-date on the latest industry news, which can gain you a lot of credibility as a team player. Remember though, when you send an article out to your team, make sure you anticipate any questions that may come up about what you sent.

4. Be Proactive

Sometimes you can't wait for someone else to give you the green light. Take initiative, and do what needs to be done before someone asks you (or someone else) to do it. Start by identifying tasks that are falling through the cracks and completing them. Your foresight will be appreciated.

5. Start With the Fun Stuff

Lastly, some workplaces have extracurricular activities you can get involved in, be it the softball team or the sustainability initiative. Show your leadership skills there and get to know more people at work as a first step towards more official responsibility. Plus, it can be good for your co-workers to get to know you outside of your traditional professional environment.

Are you stalled in a project at work, waiting on someone else to take initiative to get things moving? Are you in a broken professional relationship — with a manager, coworker, or employee — hoping the other person assumes blame and fixes the issue? Are you looking for an easy way to get focused or improve your productivity — a silver bullet from an unexpected source?

One of the most common momentum killers I've seen in my professional life is our propensity to wait for someone else to act, take initiative, assume blame, or take charge. But very often, no help comes.

In a world where problems are getting more complex, determined and innovative problem-solving will flow from those who live as if help is not coming. Living with responsibility can make us stronger and more action-oriented individuals. It's up to you to make change and take responsibility for outcomes in your professional life.   What are you waiting for?

What is responsible behavior?

Some might think that being responsible is the same thing as being accountable. But my later research suggests these are quite different mindsets. Being accountable means you are answerable and willing to accept the outcomes or results of a project or activity. But responsibility goes much further. It is the mindset that says, "I am the person who must make this happen," whether it stems from your belief or because your job requires this of you, or there is some social force binding you to this obligation.

Accountability: The Secret Sauce of Responsibility

Clearly defining responsibility is certainly essential, but encouraging people to go a step further to get personally involved will secure better results every time. That's where taking accountability comes into play. The notion of "taking accountability" naturally sounds more significant than "having responsibility"—you're making the choice to go beyond what you're responsible for, carrying with it an idea of ownership, involvement, and engagement. Earlier we looked at how a responsible team or organization might function. Now, let's look at an accountable team or organization. In a workplace culture where this positive and empowering version of accountability is embraced, you'll find that:

- People at all levels take ownership for the strategic results of the organization.
- Balls do not get dropped and projects do not slip through the cracks.
- People think differently about the job that needs to get done.
- People break-down barriers and collaborate to achieve the right results.

Why? Because accountability is a broader concept than responsibility—it's something you do to yourself, not something that someone does to you. It's with this version of accountability that people not only take accountability for the results they need to achieve individually but for results that they are not 100% in control of. Organizations embracing positive accountability have a culture of people that hold themselves accountable for the ultimate results of the organization.

Getting Positive Accountability

It's not hard to see that the prevailing notions of accountability need to be fixed—we need something more positively defined as "a personal choice to rise above one's circumstances and demonstrate the ownership necessary for achieving desired results." When you shift mindsets, and thought processes this way, you'll begin to see and feel traction in yourself and in others. Over nearly three decades of working with some of the world's top organizations and leaders, we've observed 16 Accountability Traits that are the essence of "taking accountability."

Accountable individuals, teams, and organizations are good at:

1. Obtaining the perspective of others
2. Communicating openly and candidly
3. Asking for and offering feedback
4. Hearing and saying the hard things to see reality
5. Being personally invested
6. Learning from both successes and failures
7. Ensuring my work is aligned with Key Results
8. Acting on the feedback I (we) receive
9. Constantly asking "What else can I (we) do?"
10. Collaborating across functional boundaries
11. Creatively dealing with obstacles
12. Taking the necessary risks
13. Doing the things, I (we) say I (we) will do
14. Staying "Above The Line®" by not blaming others
15. Tracking progress with proactive and transparent reporting
16. Building an environment of trust

    These traits have proven, over time, as being the mandatory actions that create the process of taking positive accountability. Adopt the right mindset and step up to these traits and you'll quickly realize that accountability is not assigned, not put upon, not, at times, so exactly defined that it creates silos, finger pointing, and the blame game. It is chosen.

Curiosity & "Thank You" goes a long way

Happiness is a good thing. Yet, both in my professional research and in my personal experience, I've observed that when we focus solely on what we think will make us happy, we can lose track of what actually does.

For most of us, the answer is no. The majority of Americans spend less than 20 percent of each day doing what could be termed very engaging, enjoyable and meaningful activities (such as talking with close friends, bonding with loved ones, creating, playing, or pursuing a spiritual practice). Instead, most of our time and energy are spent either engaged in unsatisfying work activities and chores (commuting, standing in line at the post office, fixing broken appliances), or decompressing in ways that bring neither joy nor challenge (watching TV, snacking or just "doing nothing").

It doesn't have to be this way, though — if we're willing to shake up our pursuit of happiness by introducing some elements of surprise.

One of the most reliable and overlooked keys to happiness is cultivating and exercising our innate sense of curiosity. That's because curiosity — a state of active interest or genuinely wanting to know more about something — creates an openness to unfamiliar experiences, laying the groundwork for greater opportunities to experience discovery, joy and delight.

Curiosity is something that can be nurtured and developed. With practice, we can harness the power of curiosity to transform everyday tasks into interesting and enjoyable experiences. We can also use curiosity to intentionally create wonder, intrigue and play out of almost any situation or interaction we encounter.

It all starts with wanting to know more.

Here are five of the important ways that curiosity enhances our well-being and the quality of our lives:

1. Health

In a 1996 study published in Psychology and Aging, more than 1,000 older adults aged 60 to 86 were carefully observed over a five-year period, and researchers found that those who were rated as being more curious at the beginning of the study were more likely to be alive at its conclusion, even after taking into account age, whether they smoked, the presence of cancer or cardiovascular disease, and so on.

It is possible that declining curiosity is an initial sign of neurological illness and declining health. Nonetheless, there are promising signs that enhancing curiosity reduces the risk for these diseases and may even reverse some of the natural degeneration that occurs in older adults.

2. Intelligence

Studies have shown that curiosity positively correlates with intelligence. Other studies have shown that high levels of curiosity in adults are connected to greater analytic ability, problem-solving skills and overall intelligence. All of which suggests that cultivating more curiosity in your daily life is likely to make you smarter.

3. Social Relationships

It is far easier to form and maintain satisfying, significant relationships when you demonstrate an attitude of openness and genuine interest. One of the top reasons why couples seek counseling or therapy is because they've become bored with each other. This often sparks resentment, hostility, communication breakdowns and a lack of interest in spending time together (only adding to the initial problem). Curious people report more satisfying relationships and marriages. Happy couples describe their partners as interested and responsive.

Curious people are inclined to act in ways that allow relationships to develop more easily. In one of my studies, participants spent five minutes getting acquainted with a stranger of the opposite sex, and each person made judgments about his or her partner's personality. We also interviewed their closest friends and parents to gain added insight into the qualities that curious people bring to relationships. Each of these groups — acquaintances of a mere five minutes, close friends and parents — characterized curious people as highly enthusiastic and energetic, talkative, interesting in what they say and do, displaying a wide range of interests, confident, humorous, less likely to express insecurities, and lacking in timidity and anxiety compared with less curious people. Curious people ask questions and take an interest in learning about partners, and they intentionally try to keep interactions interesting and playful. This approach supports the development of good relationships.

4. Happiness

The Gallup organization recently reported the results of a survey conducted with more than 130,000 people from some 130 nations, a sample designed to represent 96 percent of the world's population. The poll identified two factors that had the strongest influence on how much enjoyment a person experienced in a given day: "being able to count on someone for help" and "learned something yesterday."

What this poll confirms is that developing good relationships with other people (see above) and growing as a person are foundational components of a "happy" life. Both factors are supported by curiosity.

5. Meaning

If we are going to find a meaningful purpose or calling in life, chances are good we will find it in something that unleashes our natural curiosity and fascination. Indeed, curiosity is the entry point to many of life's greatest sources of meaning and satisfaction: our interests, hobbies and passions.

While being passionate about something naturally renders you curious to know as much as you can about it, it also works the other way around: The more curiosity you can muster for something, the more likely you are to notice and learn about it, and thus the more interesting and meaningful it will become for you over time.

This is true of people, books, sports, skills and conversations. Often, the more curiosity and energy we invest in exploring and understanding them, the more compelling they become. This has important implications for how much meaning and passion we experience in life: The greater the range and depth of our curiosity, the more opportunities we have to experience things that inspire and excite us, from minute details to momentous occasions.

Tune in to Your Curiosity

One of the best ways to better appreciate the power of curiosity is to start exercising it more consciously in your daily experiences. By doing so, you can transform routine tasks, enlivening them with new energy. You will also likely begin to notice more situations that have the potential to engage you, giving your curiosity even more opportunities to flourish.

KEY #5 - COMMIT TO EXCELLENCE

Exceptionality at its Best

I am a big fan of people who want to be the best of the best at what they do. They want to do it so well that no one in history has ever come to do what they have done as well as they have and no one to come after them can do the same. We can only name a few people in history who are exemplar of this.

Most people who have "made it" and made the successful strides to move forward in extraordinary excellence have mastered their craft. They can do what they do in their sleep without hesitation. They may be a fly by night sensation but they worked at what they have.

So, let's just go ahead and get one thing out of the way: The Truth

HARD WORK PAYS OFF

Malcolm Galdwell once said that 10,000 hours of practice can make you an expert. If you keep trying at it, you will make it.

Here are some steps to take to reach exceptionality at its best with what you do. are some things you need to work on:

1. Work On Yourself, Not On Your Job

Your work is a reflection of you. If you're not getting the results you're looking for, stop looking for better strategies. Instead, look inside.

Are you currently the person who would *attract* the level of success you seek? Your outer conditions are a reflection of your inner reality. If you want something different: improve you. Most people focus on their craft or their "job." That's all well and good. However, you'll get far more bang-for-your-buck by focusing on yourself and your craft.
20% of your energy should be devoted to your work. 80% of your energy should be devoted to rest and self-improvement. This is what fuels your work and makes it better than anyone else's. Self-improvement is more than books and true rest is renewal.
  While others are trying to improve their job, you're continuously improving yourself, expanding your vision, skills, and abilities. Within a short period of time, you'll have developed true mastery. Everyone else is trying to hone their "craft." Don't work on your job. Work on yourself.
  When you do, your work will far exceed what other people are painstakingly producing. Your work will be cleaner, clearer, and more powerful because you'll be more evolved as a person. Most people you're "competing" against are an inner mess.

2. Consistently Put Yourself Into Situations Others Can Only Dream Of

Your results aren't a reflection of your talent. Lots of people have talent. Few people, however, are required to rise to a difficult challenge.
  Most people never put themselves in demanding situations--situations that humble and scare you.
  You need to put yourself into positions that create

immense pressure. The kind of pressure that will either make or break you. This is how you purge out your weakness and small-mindedness. It won't be pretty. But it will change you. And eventually, you'll rise up. New. Changed. Better.

You need to be taking on challenges that require you to become so much more than you currently are. You need to put your back against the wall so you have no other choice but to produce.

This is how you evolve.

How do you put yourself into these situations? You initiate. You don't wait for life to come to you. You don't wait for the "next" opportunity. You improve your current situation or "job" by providing actual value. You pitch ideas. You ask questions. You try and fail. You take on roles that require greater responsibility.

"Leadership" is available to everyone. You just need to assume a leadership *role*. You can do that right now, in whatever situation you're in. You do this enough, and continuously pitch yourself and your ideas, you'll *create* opportunities. You then maximize those opportunities and more will come.

Opportunities are like ideas. The more you use them, rather than let them simmer, the more will come. Most people sit on their ideas far too long and they become stale. Similarly, most people sit on their opportunities too long and they stop coming.

3. Don't Copy Other People. Make Them Copy You.

If you're still mimicking the work of other people, good luck.
If you're trying to replicate the work and results of *other people*, what does that say about your own inner compass?

What does that say about your motivations?
Are you just trying to find what's working?
Are you looking for the "how"?
Do you actually know where you're going?

If you're following someone else's tracks, where do you think those tracks will lead you? To your own destination or to theirs?

And even if you'd be happy with their destination, do you really think you could do it better than them? It's *their path.* They're driven by something deep and internal. You can't get ahead if you're always a few steps behind. If you're always reacting rather than creating.

If you don't know who you are, you'll always try to be someone else. And thus, you'll never be the best. Your work will always be a cheap imitation. It will lack the *feeling* that produced the work or the idea.

4. Stay In Love With The Process

The process--or the work itself--is all there is. Results come and go. And it's never been about the results. Success is inevitable.

Success comes easy because it's the last thing on your mind. You already know it's going to happen.

The work itself--and becoming better and better at it--is what drives you. It almost doesn't matter *what* you're doing. It's *why* you're doing it that matters.

The "what" can and does take many forms. Don't over-attach to one role. Whether you're a leader, writer, athlete, parent, "employee"--the what doesn't matter. Why you do it and subsequently how you do it is what matters. Hence, how you do anything is how you do everything.

When you are in love with the process, you seek feedback, mentoring, and coaching--even when you're at the top of your game.

You surround yourself with people who aren't afraid to tell you the truth. You avoid people who suck-up and only tell you what they think you want to hear. Those aren't friends. They have an agenda. Self-transcendence comes from collaborating with others who are driven by a greater and grander vision. When the whole becomes fundamentally different than the sum of its parts. When the work is the reward.

Going beyond anything you've ever imagined. Complete openness to the possibilities. Unless you're continuously improving and working with better people, you'll never realize this.

When you hone yourself, your work, and you produce -- opportunities will come. They won't help but come. Because you're a magnet, pulling them in.

5. Never Forget Why You're Doing This

It blows me away how often I see people throw their value-systems out the door in hopes for quick success.

When I see this happen, I already know these people won't succeed long-term. They clearly don't have a "why" -- or they forgot it. They don't have an inner compass. Consequently, they don't really know where they're headed. It's a destructive path.

The moment you start compromising, you won't stop compromising. In our minds, we can justify these small choices. None of those things, when they first happen, feels like a life-changing decision. The marginal costs are almost always low. But each of those decisions can roll up into a much bigger picture, turning you into the kind of person you never wanted to be.

This, unfortunately, is more common than not.

It's so common, in fact, that it's almost expected. Hence, few people become the best at what they do. They end up becoming something far less.

Innovation vs. Imagination

Imagination and innovation are not the same. **Imagination is the root of innovation.** Like any toolbox, our minds have an assortment of tools available for us to utilize whenever we need to.
Included in our mental toolbox are cognitive processes, clusters of which compose of three primary ones involved in ideation: imagination, creativity, and innovative thinking.
Unless we know the differences between the tools at our disposal, we may find ourselves attempting to hammer in a nail using a screwdriver. It might get the job done, but it's definitely not ideal.
Imagination is about seeing the impossible, or unreal. Creativity is using imagination to unleash the potential of existing ideas in order to create new and valuable ones. Innovation is taking existing, reliable systems and ideas and improving them.
Typically, we often confuse these three for one or the other. Dreams at night are a type of imaginative thinking; what you see when you dream isn't really happening, and in most instances what you dream cannot physically happen. A great example of this is a recurring dream I have, where a blue-colored cat teaches me how to fly.

When solving a novel problem at work or school, we rely on creativity to generate an answer or idea for overcoming the problem. We might know what the problem entails, but we can only solve it by combining ideas or diverging from our focus in order to see what we couldn't see before. Creativity very much deals with reality, but the solutions we generate as a result of creativity are difficult to measure.

Lastly, innovation is what takes place when we look at an existing system or process and find a way to improve it, often utilizing both imagination and creativity.

The biggest difference between each of these is the <u>frame of focus</u> we have when attempting to utilize each. With imagination, our focus can be on things that are impossible. Creativity requires our focus to be on things that *might* be possible, but we can't be sure until we explore them further. While innovation entails being focused on what is right in front of us, something that can be measurably improved in the here and now.

It's important to know the differences, and to know when you're using one mode of thinking as opposed to the other, and what the context is for that reasoning.

Where imagination simply requires that we have *some* context from which to envision an idea, creativity requires that we have knowledge of the idea, motivation and freedom to explore and tinker, intelligence to see what makes the convergence of any set of ideas possible, and then the energy to see the process through.

Innovation takes both creativity and imagination further, focusing on existing systems or ideas that can be evolved naturally.

Where imagination can tell a remarkable story, creativity can make imagination possible. Innovation uses imagination and the power of creativity to measurable improve on what exists today.

If you're trying to improve a process or idea at work or school, you should focus on thinking with innovation in mind. Innovation is the way to see how something might work in the future.

If, alternatively, you're looking to generate a new way to solve a problem in your life, utilizing creative thinking is the way to go. Be sure, in those instances, you have everything you need to think creatively.

Lastly, if you want to see things from an entirely different perspective, work to build your imagination.

While growing up, I was fortunate to find myself surrounded by designers, writers, educators, and artists. It was incredible to watch them work, to generate shapes and words and entire ideas from seemingly nothing.

As I grew older and began my career in design, I found myself driven toward questions around what it means to be creative and why the same modes of thinking—of generating ideas and concepts from nothing—aren't typically celebrated in non-artistic or non-entrepreneurial fields.

So, I started digging into research not only on creative thinking, but sociology and psychology. I would read endless books, one after the other.

I would come to learn that **creativity isn't what I had been led to think it was.** Creativity isn't a magical or mystical force, it isn't a "gift" that some have and others don't. Creativity is a process of thinking that relies on multiple factors.

This led to a big problem. If creativity is something we're born with (or not born with) or something a fortunate few stumbles onto in their life, then it's easy to dismiss it as something each of us doesn't need to pursue. If I don't feel particularly creative I can simply brush it off as "I'm just not the creative type."

But the facts from research starting back in the 1950s has shown repeatedly: creativity is a process of thinking.

Robert Senberg says:
"Creativity requires a confluence of six distinct but interrelated resources: **1. intellectual abilities***,* **2. knowledge***,* **3. styles of thinking***,* **4. personality***,* **5. motivation***, and* **6. environment***. Although levels of these resources are sources of individual differences, often the decision to use a resource is a more important source of*

individual differences."

What Sternberg goes on to explain is that creativity requires a deliberate decision to optimize and utilize these resources in our lives. Creativity is a conscious choice we make, or don't. All it takes is purposefully deciding to use these resources in your own life.

For example: You can be remarkably intelligent, but if you're unmotivated or if you live in an environment that discourages creative exploration, you may be able to solve complex problems, but you are unlikely to solve complex problems in areas you have little knowledge in.

Similarly, if you're weak in one resource but more competent in two others, those resources can make up for the lack in the first. So, if you're not particularly intelligent but you often use a thinking style of dedicating yourself to an idea while also knowing a lot about the subject category, you're more likely to stumble onto creative output than if you were weak in all of those areas.

This is great news in our search to understand and utilize creative thinking. The theory means that we are in more control of our creativity than historians and critics would have had us believe!

We can often influence our environment, seeking out one online (for example) that encourages ideation and exploration. We can modify our thinking styles to be more globally-oriented as well: thinking not only about the immediate impact of ideas, but seeing the larger, global impact as well. Knowledge we can also easily gain, by reading, traveling, or conversing with others.

If we are lacking in one resource we can focus our efforts on strengthening it or relying on other resources to make up for it.

To be creative, according to this research, is a conscious choice we must make.

The important factor to being creative is not merely dedicating ourselves to thinking in new ways, but in doing so decisively and on both small (or local) and large (or global) scales.

This is where many people drop the ball. They come up with an idea and run with it without giving much additional thought to it. They accept solutions outright and accept the first reasonable conclusion.
And, really, much of our global culture promotes this type of behavior. Think: get rich quick schemes, the drive-thru or microwave meals, television that not only entertains, but does so in a way that means you don't have to think very much about what it is your eyes are absorbing.

    This is what makes us as creatives so valuable. We are unique, not because we have an innate gift that is rare to us, but because we are the ones who have decisively (though sometimes unconsciously) decided to use the resources available to us in order to think in new ways. Where others might reject an idea, or move onto something else early-on in a process, we are the ones who work through the ideas more and more until we end up in a place where suddenly others want to "buy" the idea.

Imagination is the realm of the mind where you see things that do not yet exist in this world, but which one day might. It is an under-appreciated yet critical element of creativity and innovation.

    Children, writers, artists and musicians are perceived as having the greatest imaginations. The novelist has to create in her mind characters, location, actions and plot. A great composer has to hear in her mind the interaction of many musical instruments in order to create a piece that stirs emotion.

    Imagination is not a word you hear much about in business. Few companies, outside electronic game producers, would describe themselves as imaginative. That is a shame and a mistake. Imagination is the number one tool for creativity and innovation.
Over the past couple of years, "innovation" has become an incredibly catchy business term. Every business aims to be innovative. Every business knows that it needs to innovate to grow.

Likewise, creativity is an admired skill in business these days. Once only advertising people were expected to be creative. Today, most businesses seek creative people. And that makes sense. Innovation is creativity implemented. So, if you want to run an innovative company, you need creative people. Imagination, however, is not a word you hear much about in business. Few companies, outside electronic game producers, would describe themselves as imaginative.

"Without imagination, people can not look at problems from new perspectives."

Learn from your mistakes

The most important life lessons we will ever learn will be from the bad decisions we make. Time and experience can be excellent teachers when you actually learn a lesson from your poor decisions. Experience comes from our way of living, understanding and the adjustments we make. It also comes from suffering, agony and the ordeals we are afflicted by.

We need to learn from our mistakes so that we do not run the risk of repeating them. We must develop the wisdom and sense to make good decisions and choices. Good judgment will only develop if you truly learn from your mistakes. Unfortunately, for many people, it takes a few repeats of the same mistake to learn the lesson.

Good or bad, experiences are what help us learn lessons and form a better sense of judgment. Bad judgment seems to stick with us longer as a lesson learned because we really do not want to keep repeating it. Wisdom is the knowledge you can gain from making mistakes.

I wholeheartedly believe that good judgment comes from experimentation with life. That includes poor decisions and bad judgment to ensure that good judgment might be recognized by a person and will remain a permanent fixture in their lives. If you have a difficult time making decisions or always blame your bad outcomes on others, then you have not learned anything. If you have not learned from anything, you will continue to have bad experiences that will cause you to make more poor judgments. Until you realize that, you will continue to suffer.

You can only learn from the error of your ways if you recognize the   fact that you messed up; Too many people remain in denial and place the blame on others. The minute you take responsibility for yourself is when the learning process will begin. When you admit your mistakes, you hasten your learning development.

  Everything we are exposed to in life presents us with another valuable lesson. Not only can you learn from your own experiences, but also the experiences of the people you surround yourself with. Sometimes these can serve as the most meaningful lessons since it allows you to observe behaviors from an objective standpoint.

Growth starts as soon as you recognize your mistake and how to prevent it from happening again. Everyone makes mistakes in life, this is normal, but how you learn from them is how you develop your judgment. The only way to prevent making a mistake a second time is to learn. If you don't, you will be making that same error again and again until you are forced to learn.

  Some mistakes can be lethal, some can cost you money or friends, and some are inconsequential and could be ignored. Regardless of what type of error you made, it needs to be acknowledged and analyzed to prevent it from occurring again. The lessons lie in the way we interpret our errors. If you keep repeating the same patterns, how can you ever expect your results to differ? It is much more beneficial to face the mistake than to escape from it because it will never be solved by itself. Looking at mistakes and working toward understanding them will promote progress and insight. It is normal to feel shameful about an error you have made, but you cannot hide in denial. If you do that, your progress will only be hindered.

  You can only learn from a mistake after you admit you've made it. As soon as you start blaming other people (or the universe itself) you distance yourself from any possible lesson. But if you courageously stand up and honestly say "This is my mistake and I am responsible" the possibilities for learning will move towards you. Admission of a mistake, even if only privately to yourself, makes learning possible by moving the focus away from blame assignment and towards understanding. Wise people admit their mistakes easily. They know progress accelerates when they do.

This advice runs counter to the cultural assumptions we have about mistakes and failure, namely that they are shameful things. We're taught in school, in our families, or at work to feel guilty about failure and to do whatever we can to avoid mistakes. This sense of shame combined with the inevitability of setbacks when attempting difficult things explains why many people give up on their goals: they're not prepared for the mistakes and failures they'll face on their way to what they want. What's missing in many people's beliefs about success is the fact that the more challenging the goal, the more frequent and difficult setbacks will be. The larger your ambitions, the more dependent you will be on your ability to overcome and learn from your mistakes.

But for many reasons admitting mistakes is difficult. An implied value in many cultures is that our work represents us: if you fail a test, then you are a failure. If you make a mistake then you are a mistake (You may never have felt this way, but many people do. It explains the behavior of some of your high school or college friends). Like eggs, steak and other tasty things we are given letter grades (A, B, C, D and F) organizing us for someone else's consumption: universities and employers evaluate young candidates on their grades, numbers based on scores from tests unforgiving to mistakes.

For anyone than never discovers a deeper self-identity, based not on lack of mistakes but on courage, compassionate intelligence, commitment and creativity, life is a scary place made safe only by never getting into trouble, never breaking rules and never taking the risks that their hearts tell them they need to take.

Learning from mistakes requires three things:

-Putting yourself in situations where you can make interesting mistakes
-Having the self-confidence to admit to them
-Being courageous about making changes

    Learning from mistakes that fall into the first two categories (Stupid & Simple) is easy, but shallow. Once you recognize the problem and know the better way, you should be able to avoid similar mistakes. Or in some cases you'll realize that no matter what you do once in a while you'll do stupid things (e.g. even Einstein stubbed his toes).

    But these kinds of mistakes are not interesting. The lessons aren't deep and it's unlikely they lead you to learn much about yourself or anything else. For example, compare these two mistakes

    The kind of mistakes you make define you. The more interesting the mistakes, the more interesting the life. If your biggest mistakes are missing reruns of television shows or buying the wrong lottery ticket you're not challenging yourself enough to earn more interesting mistakes.

    And since there isn't much to learn from simple and stupid mistakes, most people try to minimize their frequency and how much time we spend recovering from them. Their time is better spent learning from bigger mistakes. But if we habitually or compulsively make stupid mistakes, then what we really have is an involved mistake.

    The biggest lesson to learn in involved mistakes is that you have to examine your own ability to change. Some kinds of change will be easier for you than others and until you make mistakes and try to correct them you won't know which they are.

    You learn how to handle a complex mistake. The most interesting kinds of mistake are the last group: Complex mistakes. The more complicated the mistake you've made, the more patient you need to be. There's nothing worse than flailing around trying to fix something you don't understand: you'll always make things worse.

Another major lesson in all of mistake making is to trust that while mistakes are inevitable, if you can learn from the current one, you'll also be able to learn from future ones. No matter what happens tomorrow you'll be able to get value from it, and apply it to the day after that. Progress won't be a straight line but if you keep learning you will have more successes than failures, and the mistakes you make along the way will help you get to where you want to go.

Here's your checklist for you to check things off along the way.

Accepting responsibility makes learning possible.
- o Don't equate making mistakes with being a mistake.
- o You can't change mistakes, but you can choose how to respond to them.
- o Growth starts when you can see room for improvement.
- o Work to understand why it happened and what the factors were.
- o What information could have avoided the mistake?
- o What small mistakes, in sequence, contributed to the bigger mistake?
- o Are there alternatives you should have considered but did not?
- o What kinds of changes are required to avoid making this mistake again?
- o What kinds of change are difficult for you?
- o How do you think your behavior should/would change in you were in a similar situation again?
- o Work to understand the mistake until you can make fun of it (or not want to kill others that make fun).
- o Don't over-compensate: the next situation won't be the same as the last.

You can only learn from a mistake after you admit you've made it. As soon as you start blaming other people (or the universe itself), you distance yourself from any possible lesson. But if you courageously stand up and honestly say "This is my mistake and I am responsible" the possibilities for learning will move towards you. Admission of a mistake, even if only privately to yourself, makes learning possible by moving the focus away from blame assignment and towards understanding. Wise people admit their mistakes easily. They know progress accelerates when they do.

Stop being nice to yourself

    I have been told how nice I am my entire life. This is usually a great compliment to me. I love it when people tell me I'm nice, because I *am* nice. In fact, throughout my life I've tried my best to be kind, caring, empathetic and helpful to just about everyone I meet. These qualities are the bedrock on which much of my identity is based.
    I have learned over the years though that "nice" is good, but "too nice" is not. "Too nice" is the person who doesn't like to ruffle feathers. "Too nice" is the person who is afraid to set boundaries. "Too nice" is the person who is afraid to say no. "Too nice" is the person who I used to be (and still am, sometimes).
    When I reflect back on my life and my various relationships — with people, I can now see how being "too nice" was my way of staying safe, of avoiding conflict, and of remaining emotionally intact.
    It takes a lot of effort to say yes, when we really mean no, to say we're okay, when we're really not, to always focus on the other person's needs, when we have a boatload of needs of our own. So, after a season of being "too nice," there was always that inevitable point where I exhausted myself, where I couldn't go on another minute without rest. And since I did not understand the nature of my fears, and I could not see a way out of my self-imposed bondage, the only option I could ever

envision was retreating, so that I could go to my alone room, and be who I really was.

My greatest challenge is remembering every day to rest in the knowledge that as an adult, it is no longer possible for me to be engulfed, as I was when I was a child. I am a powerful presence even when I'm not trying to be, and I no longer need to retreat to be who I really am. In fact, none of us do.

1. You Say "Sorry" On Repeat

If you did something wrong, or are canceling plans, then it makes sense to say sorry. But nice people tend to get carried away with the word. Everything becomes "sorry this" and "sorry that," often to the point where it loses its meaning. And when that happens, you're not doing anyone any favors by asking for forgiveness, according to an article on EliteDaily.com. You're simply trying to appease your own (often imagined) guilt.

2. Your Needs Are Never Met

Nice people tend to attract users — partners who are lazy, friends who always need help moving, family members who constantly have a favor to ask. It's OK to be helpful, but it crosses over into bad territory when these people are never there for you in return. "If you bend over backwards over and over and never get anything in return, you're acting like a doormat, not being nice," said Elizabeth Stone on ThoughtCatalog.com.

3. You Feel Resentful After You Say "Yes"

I'll say it again — there's nothing wrong with being nice. The only time it's bad is when you it brings on a sense of resentment, or overwhelm. "To know if you've crossed that fine line from kind to compulsive people-pleaser, pay attention to how you feel — in the moment and later," said Kate Lowenstein on HuffingtonPost.com, in an interview with psychologist Linda Tillman, Ph.D. If you feel a burning sense of resentment after agreeing to something, then it's a good sign you said yes out of obligation, and not because you actually wanted to.

4. You Never Voice Your Opinion

Think about your group of friends. Who is it that chooses the restaurant, movie, or vacation spot? Not you? Then you might have a problem.

5. You Agree Without Thinking

Do you ever agree to something and then think, "Wait, why did I just say that?" It is possible to get in the habit of constantly nodding in agreement, and saying yes to everything. It's an admirable trait, but not something that is sustainable for very long.

6. You Don't Have Your Own Life

When it comes to jobs, relationships, friendships, etc., it's absolutely necessary that you have your own life outside of them. Nice people, however, tend to get 100 percent absorbed in such things, to the point they no longer have their own life.

7. You Avoid Confrontation At All Costs

Very few people actually enjoy fighting, so it's perfectly normal to avoid arguments and confrontation. What's not normal? Being a total doormat because you're afraid to ruffle any feathers. It may feel like the polite thing to do, but it's not a good thing.

8. You're Afraid Of Being Rejected

A fear of rejection may be at the root of why you're so darn nice. If, for whatever reason, you feel like you don't deserve the people and things in your life, then you may do anything and everything to keep them — including being overly nice. Sound familiar?

9. Your Calendar Is Full Of Stuff You Don't Want To Do

Take a look at that planner of yours. How much of your calendar is filled up with stuff for you, versus stuff for other people? If the ratio is skewed wildly in the favor of other people, it may be a sign you're being too nice.

10. Your Friends Toss Around The Word "Codependence"

Remember what I said about nice people attracting users? This can often lead to a codependent relationship. That's where you find yourself wrapped up with someone who needs you, and you need them, in an entirely unearthly way. You might find yourself giving support to your partner, at the expense of your own mental health. You may also stay with someone, even though the relationship is unhealthy. These are all signs of codependence.

11. You're Constantly Swamped At Work

If your boss gives you extra work, it's often a sign he or she trusts you. But it could also be that you've become their go-to workhorse, since they know you'll never say no. This can be an excellent strategy for getting ahead in your career, but it can also mean your boss may take advance of you.

And with that, you have some strategies (and good reasons) for toning down your niceness. Don't turn it off, because sweet people are awesome. The key is to stay your sweet self, while at the same time avoiding the negatives of being too nice.

KEY #6 – CENTER YOUR BALANCE

Start with a dream

Everything starts as a dream, a thought, a mental image, but this is just the first step. If you stay there, you will enjoy your dream, but one day you will see that you are standing still, like a person watching a beautiful and inspiring movie, over and again, but not going out to the real world to create and live what he or she has seen in the movie.

Are you waiting for some miracle to change your life? Sometimes, miracles do happen, but why not make the miracles happen? You can create miracles, when you know what you want, adopt a positive attitude, and take action.

Help the miracle happen, by participating in its creation, by planning, visualizing, expecting, and acting. When you contribute to making things happen, they eventually happen, sometimes quite fast, and sometimes, gradually, over a period of time.

To achieve a dream, you need to take action. For most people, it looks like a difficult step, because you don't know where to start and what to do. It is here that most people stop and don't go further. The people who succeed are those that think, plan, read, and look around them to see open doors. In order to see the open doors, you need motivation and faith in yourself.

This has to do with every area of life, including relationships, work, material success, self-improvement, meditation and spiritual growth.

Don't wait for miracles to happen. Make them happen. Everything starts as a dream, but requires action. Even miracles require some action on your part.

Do you want to make a new start? Why wait? Do you want to write the book you have always wanted to write? Do you want to learn a new language? Do you want to have a loving relationship? Do you want to start a business? Do you want to go on the trip you have always dreamed about? Do you want to learn to meditate? Take action now.

Don't be afraid of the "action" part. You can take action that takes you closer to your goals, even if you don't have enough money, time, or the proper circumstances.

Everything starts as a dream, but requires action for making it a reality. Dream, but also visualize and affirm. Visualization and affirmations are "action steps." They will open doors for you, but you need to take action to open the door and enter. Sometimes, you might find yourself pushed into an open door, toward success, but on most occasions, you will see the door and recognize it, but you need the "action part" of opening it, passing through it, and doing things to make the goal come true.

In all these steps, motivation, passion, and perseverance are of vital importance.

Don't wait for the opportunity to come. Create the opportunity. Visualize it, affirm that it is already here, and prepare yourself for it, so that when it appears, you recognize it, and take advantage of it.

Learn how to use the power of affirmations to improve your life, build good habits, increase confidence, and to attract success, love and happiness into your life. A book with all the advice and guidance you need.

Protect yourself from burnout

Burnout is defined as physical or mental collapse caused by overwork or stress. As it turns out, there are ways to identify the early warning signs of burnout. And, there are many simple practices you can put in place immediately to prevent burnout from becoming an occupational hazard .

I have burnout several times in my life. The cause is obvious but the signs are sometimes not as obvious.

Here are 13 Early Signs of Burnout:
1. High levels of stress or anxiety. Feeling frequently on edge, with adrenaline constantly coursing through your body.
2. Lack of engagement. You don't feel motivated at work. You have difficulty focusing or exhibit a short attention span.
3. Increased cynicism. Feelings of resentment or disconnection. You may notice yourself being more negative and cynical. Feeling cranky and defensive or snapping at people easily. You don't make time to talk on the phone or connect with the people who matter most to you. If you're feeling a lot of resentment towards others, chances are it's because you're not getting your needs met and you're on the path to burnout.
4. Distracted eating. You eat your meals in front of a computer, television or while on the go (in the car, standing up, etc.)

5. **Not getting enough sleep.** The suggested minimum amount of sleep is seven to eight hours each night, if you're getting less than this, you risk some level of burn out.

6. **Low energy and exhaustion.** You're tired. Not just sleepy tired, but emotionally fatigued. You may feel exhausted by the end of the day, with no energy left to exercise or even engage with others, you just want to crash and watch television or zone out in some other way.

7. **Never enough time.** You feel as though you're always in a hurry and never have enough time for all the things you're trying to accomplish each day.

8. **Excessive worrying, high level of self-criticism.** Your mind cycles through the same worry filled thoughts again and again and you can't seem to stop. The critical voice in your head is very loud, telling you constantly to do more, work harder, and no matter what you accomplish, you're still not doing enough. There is no self-compassionate voice to balance out the critical voice, or if there is, it is very weak and you can barely hear it.

9. **Physical illness.** Initially, the physical symptoms can be subtle. You may experience headaches, a persistent cold, have a stomach bug or an upset stomach frequently, or a weak immune system in general. If early signs are ignored, your body may hit a wall and receive a more serious diagnosis.

10. **Numb feelings.** Increase in addictive behavior. Initially, this can show up as an excessive dependence on caffeine and/or sugar to stay alert and boost energy when feeling low. As things progress, an increased dependence on drugs, alcohol, eating comfort foods or watching more television than usual can be signs you're burning out and using these coping mechanisms to avoid acknowledging how you really feel.

11. **Inefficacy.** Experiencing diminished personal accomplishment, a perceived decline in competence or productivity, and expending energy at work without seeing any results.

12. **No Breaks.**
- **Vacation.** You can't remember the last time you took a single day off just to relax and do nothing. Or perhaps you haven't

had a vacation in over six or even twelve months.
- Recharge throughout the day. You may have a tendency to push through your work without taking a break. It's one thing to be in the zone, but if you notice you're not getting up to get a glass of water, stretch your legs, go on a walk or call a friend at least once every 90-120 minutes, you could be putting unnecessary stress on your body.
- Weekly Rituals. You haven't made time for a rejuvenating activity in the last week (massage or any pampering treatment, a bath, cooking or reading a book simply for pleasure, going on a hike, etc.).
13. Not enough exercise. You aren't making as much time to exercise or move your body as you would like.

What are some practical, simple & cost free anti burnout things to do?

First, go through the list above and circle your top three symptoms. Next, ask yourself "Hmmm, what do I need?" for each of these areas. For example, if you're eating at your desk five days a week, what you need could be to connect with friends or colleagues over lunch more often, or to exercise during your lunch break. If you haven't taken a vacation in over a year, what you need could be to schedule a vacation.

Once you determine what you need, come up with an action step for each of these three areas. An action step has a "What" and a "By When." For example, Action Step: I will plan a vacation and book the tickets by next Thursday at 4pm. Setting concrete goals is one of the best ways to ensure you'll make a change.

Avoiding burnout starts by putting some of these preventative measures in place. If you want even more accountability, you can recruit an *anti-burnout partner*. Tell this person what your action steps are and ask him or her to hold you accountable by checking in to make sure you've followed through. Getting support and setting clear action steps will help you implement these simple practices with greater ease.

You can "protect the asset" by taking care of your body, mind and spirit. As leaders, we often forget that we are not invincible. We do need time by ourselves where we can recharge and take care of essentials without being influenced by what is going on around us. The list below identifies some simple steps you can take to protect yourself against fatigue and burnout.

1. **Body** – we have nothing without our health. Without good health, it is hard to enjoy our family, friends and the fruits of our labor. We take our health for granted when we are healthy and then it's all we can think about when we are not healthy! That's so backwards! We should always focus on maintaining good health so that we don't have self-imposed health related events. There are literally thousands of books written on this subject but I think it is quite simple. It is critical for each of us to:
2. **Mind** – if you are not growing, you are shrinking. If you are shrinking, your leadership ability is diminishing. As leaders, we each need to continue to challenge and stretch our minds every day. Set aside 20 to 30 minutes a day for learning. Besides formal education or training in your area of expertise, you can "stretch your mind" by:
3. **Spirit** – although my worldview is Christian, and that comes with a certain set of beliefs, the term "spirit" does not necessarily have a religious connotation. If your worldview is atheist or something other than Christian, that should not discount this point. Everyone has a "spirit" that needs to be nurtured and refreshed. The following activities are spirit or soul refreshers that everyone can benefit from:

Don't forget to protect yourself from the onslaught of the everyday. This is an easy trap to fall into gradually without realizing what's happening until it is too late and the damage is done. Do a self-assessment today. What actions do you need to take to ensure that you are "protecting the asset?"

Plan, Plan, Plan

Learning how to plan — especially if you're new to organizing your time — can be a frustrating experience. And for some individuals, the reason could be their brains.

As a time, management coach, I've seen some incredibly intelligent people struggle to plan. For example, very creative people who think in pictures can initially have a difficult time translating their conceptual ideas into practical actions that then find a space on their calendars. They need someone to guide them step-by-step on how to go through this process. Or some individuals who do an amazing job on identifying and executing on their top priority can falter when it comes to tracking and completing other tasks concurrently, including managing others.

What I have discovered is that some people's brains are naturally wired for maintaining order, while others aren't.

It all comes down to brain science. Those with natural brain dominance in the back-left part of the brain are most comfortable making linear plans and following them. These individuals typically don't have a need for my coaching help and often don't understand why others struggle. But those with brain dominance in a different quadrant of their brain will find planning much harder. That's because the neurochemistry of their brain causes them to use 100 times the energy to think in "planning" mode as someone whose natural dominance is back left.

Recognize your natural strengths and weaknesses. If you find planning extremely difficult, you likely don't have natural brain dominance in the back-left part of your brain. To find out what part of your brain dominates, do the self-assessment in the book *Thriving in Mind* or participate in the more formal Benziger Thinking Styles Assessment. Learning this can help you better understand what works for you and then use that to adjust your habits. By taking the *Thriving in Mind* self-assessment, for example, I gained clarity on why certain types of work came so naturally to me and why I found myself avoiding other types of tasks.

Accept the difficulty. If we think something should be easy when it's hard, we tend to get upset and are more likely to give up. But if we set expectations that a task will be difficult, we may still flounder, but we're more willing to work through any issues, since we understand that challenge is part of the process. When my coaching clients first start planning, they describe it as frustrating, disorienting, tiring, or even anger-inducing because they don't want to accept the limits of reality in terms of how many activities can fit in a day. The clients who accept and work through those feelings are the ones who make the most progress. They find that on the other side, they have more peace, more confidence, and more clarity on how to structure their time well.

Let go of all-or-nothing thinking. One interesting phenomenon I've observed with people whose natural brain strength is not in planning is that they tend to fall into all-or-nothing thinking. They think that they must follow their plan perfectly, or their efforts have been wasted. Or if they can't plan every day, they shouldn't plan at all. Instead, view learning as a process where improvement counts and every day matters. This will build your resilience because you won't beat yourself up as much when you deviate from your plan, and in turn, you will find it easier to get back on track.

Find systems that work. Instead of forcing yourself into an established scheduling process, find a system that works for you. For example, if you tend to have a strong tendency toward visuals (a common front-right brain dominance quality), find a way to organize that takes that preference into account. Put to-do items on sticky notes, draw on whiteboards, or use mind maps. If you love spreadsheets (often found when you have a strong front-left brain dominance), put your to-do lists and plans in Excel, or consider using apps that will allow you to track your progress in a numeric fashion. If you like to see time as a flow and rhythm (a favorite of back-right dominance), use tools like paper lists that will allow you to adapt and adjust the cadence of your day as needed, instead of feeling boxed into rigid time frames. There is no wrong way to plan. Experiment until you find the right fit.

Borrow other people's brains. If you know people who excel in planning or have organization skills, ask for their advice and insight. They may be able to easily offer potential solutions to problems that overwhelm you. Getting suggestions from others on organization systems that you can then test, instead of trying to develop your own, can save you lots of time. A few caveats: Avoid critical people who may discourage you in your learning process. Change is tough enough without being torn down. Second, ask them for *simple* solutions. Don't aim for expertise in an area when you're just learning; a basic level of knowledge is a good start.

Keep trying. One of the definitions of resilience is "the ability to spring back into shape." When you find yourself getting frustrated in the process of planning, have self-compassion when you make mistakes, refocus when you get distracted, and adjust your plan when new issues crop up. For example, you may decide to move a project you thought you would get done today to the next day. Or you may reach out to a colleague for help on getting a certain deliverable done.

Understanding what's going on in your brain as you acquire time management skills makes a dramatic difference in your ability to encourage yourself and work through frustration and roadblocks. When you convince yourself that you can change and accept that you'll need to work harder than most, you have a much higher chance of being resilient in the process of improving your planning.

Do You Know the Risks of Poor Planning?

Without a plan, you're hoping. You *hope* you understood what your boss wanted. You *hope* this feature is necessary. You *hope* this is what the client meant by "make it pop". You *hope* you'll find a way to wrap up this article coherently.

KEY #7 – KEEP YOUR FOCUS

Define your brand

In order to market anything - a product, a person, an organization or an idea - you first need to define your brand. Once you define your brand you'll be able to create a foundation for all your marketing efforts and strategies. Your brand definition serves as your measuring stick when evaluating any, and all, marketing materials and strategies. To begin the process, you'll need to answer (honestly and thoughtfully) these questions:

- ✓ What products and/or services do you offer? What are the qualities of the services and/or products offered? Be sure to be as specific as possible.
- ✓ What are the core values of your products and services? What are the core values of your company? When thinking about values, think about what's "important" to you and your audience.
- ✓ What is the mission of your company? This is often a question of ethics and standards.
- ✓ What does your company specialize in? Meaning, what is your niche?
- ✓ Who is your target market audience? Identify those attracted to your products and services.
- ✓ What is the tagline of your company? What kind of message is your tagline sending to your prospects? Keep your tagline "very" short.

Once you've answered the first six questions, create a personality for your brand or company that clearly represents your products or services. Ask, what qualities set you apart from the competition? Is the personality of your company innovative, traditional, hands-on, creative, energetic or sophisticated?

Truly defining your brand is a critical first step in developing your personal or business marketing plan. Through a continuing series of stories, we've been examining how to build a compelling brand experience that will drive customer loyalty -- highlighting the principles of big brand marketing so that small business owners can replicate those kinds of successes. But before you can start building your brand's experience for customers, you need to take some fundamental first steps to define the kind of brand you want to be.

To guide our marketing plan, we need a very well-crafted statement of the type of business we are in, the type of customers we serve and how we serve them. We have to define what we stand for and the types of products and services that our customers can expect from us. This truly is the first step in the branding process.

At first glance, defining your brand may seem easy, but it takes some soul searching, decision making and data gathering.

Take, for example, someone going into business as a lawyer. It's pretty easy to define that brand -- a person who practices law, right? But to build a brand around his practice, a lawyer needs to determine specifically what kind of law he focuses on and what kind of client he is targeting before any marketing can begin. That means thinking through what regions of the world, categories of law, style of service and other offerings he brings to the table.

When defining your brand, put as much clarity as possible into how the brand and business is described, so that you can build a specific brand experience to match it.

Here are three key steps to help you get there:

1. Make an inventory of your skills. List out what you are especially good at and what you want your customers to think of when your brand comes to mind. Your unique set of skills will form the basis of your brand definition.

2. What are your customers' needs? From your list of skills, identify those that your customers particularly need. Think through the kinds of things you do that your customers will come to you for. You should define your brand based on your ability to fulfill such demands.

3. Focus on what differentiates. It's important for your brand to be different than other similar options available to customers. Of course, your brand experience will ultimately differentiate you, but being unique starts with deciding what attributes set you apart from others. Your goal is to be different and better than your competition.
Notice the clarity in the brand definition?

While it's important to be as specific as possible, you also want to be careful not to box your business in with a tightly constrained brand definition. For example, if a hair salon only defined itself as providing "women's short haircuts," it would close itself off from business that could come from customers seeking other hair styles, salon services like coloring or straightening and other demographics like children or men.

If it makes sense to be super specific because you have identified a strong niche market, just be sure to do this consciously. I've seen many salons that specialize in just curly hair or blowouts. If the business is large enough, those could be very well-defined, successful brands. Just be careful not to define the brand too strictly, which would close out future business-building activities.

The trick is to balance specificity, focus and differentiation with the ability to expand. When defining your brand, make sure to describe the type of business in a way that allows for growth over time.

Be a leader, not a boss

We have enough bosses in the world. Will the real leaders stand up and make yourself known?!

I love working with people who make self-empowered choices over when, where, and how they work. They're entrepreneurs, like me. They don't exude dependency at every turn. And they're more rapidly gaining a diversity of experience that others seldom acquire. In fact, they're honed into high performers by an unforgiving market that spits out those who can't perform.

Bosses Demand Deference. Leaders Earn It.

In studies of authoritarianism, it becomes clear that we're misusing this word "authority"—as in "I have authority over you." Actual authority is a sum of experience, recognized by other people. It's democratic—if others don't find it in us, it isn't actually there. Authority is not a matter of title, position or strategic clout. A person speaks with authority, perhaps greater authority, because other people voluntarily feel deference to their accumulated wisdom in some practice area or context.

A person who has authority never needs to remind anyone of their competence. It's clear by the problems they tackle and the deftness with which they solve them. And this is key: authority rotates. Having it doesn't diminish it in anyone else. It's the opposite of managerial title.

A VP who is an authority on logistics is not, because she's a VP, also an authority on radio-dispatch vehicles. That's why on our teams, there's no authority by fiat—no "bossness". There's only authority from talent in a given area. The final call is made after discussion is by whoever is most authoritative in the appropriate area, whether that's a specialization or a strategic outcome. So, if there is a title, it means, "in your practice area, you'll listen, and you'll make the call."

Something like a horizontal chain of command develops. After getting the best ideas available from the team, a decision is made about a program we'll run. Those who take on parts of the program make decisions about how they'll implement those parts. The process virtually eliminates micro-management. The results are scalability, efficiency, greater satisfaction from the work, and continually enhanced skill sets.

Trusting our talent can really challenge clients that are used to an authoritarian structure. The concern is, "unless someone's giving orders, how does anyone know they're doing what they should?" The answer from my company is, "we only recruit people who don't need to be ordered to do what they should." I ask for accountability for outcomes, due dates, and taking ownership of milestones when a project is collaborative. I offer immense support. Then I look for how they will create success for us.

Simply put, leaders lead

Instead of just barking orders and expecting employees to blindly follow, leaders lead the team toward completing common goals. Leaders who connect and engage with their employees often demonstrate a willingness to also perform tasks they request of their team. Leaders are ready to advise; engage in discussion and listen to any feedback an employee has to offer.

This give-and-take approach fosters employee confidence to both follow the leader and to take risks. Leaders know that when employees are empowered, motivation is higher, productivity escalates and retention increases.

Leaders go the extra mile

One of the best things about leaders is their ability and willingness to prepare a group for the tasks at hand. If colleagues are not prepared for certain duties, leaders must be there to support, teach and back them up. Leaders know that each employee is on the team for a reason and appreciates individual efforts.

A "boss" often tells employees to complete a task but may not fully equip them for the work at hand; Too often in this scenario, employees are afraid that if they fail at a project they'll be subject to reprimand or discharge. A leader is available to guide employees through the process.

Communication is key when it comes to being a good leader. Leaders listen to their team and actively seek their thoughts on critical topics. Leaders share information, check in as needed and clearly communicate expectations. A boss does not always share information or empower the team.

A leader is willing to learn, but a boss already knows it all

A true leader is not too arrogant or embarrassed to learn from those with less seniority or status. Leaders respect the skills and experience colleagues – even junior level ones – bring to the table.
When necessary, a leader offers constructive criticism, where a boss may focus on failures without seeing them as learning opportunities.   A boss limits the creative process and self-expression, killing innovation and motivation. Inevitably, employees who fall under the management style of a boss cease to care or try because they see no value in making suggestions or questioning processes.

Even in stressful or busy times, leaders know that getting top results from the team means being aware of, and sensitive to, what employees have on their plates. Leaders recognize that their workers are skilled and knowledgeable individuals who appreciate the opportunity to express opinions and feelings in any discussion that might impact work assignments. This approach generates better workforce performance than just barking orders and assigning tasks without considering current workloads or deadlines.

Take a good look at your management style – or that of your leadership team – and the overall attitude of your staff. If it's time to make a change, leadership training is available to help. A few simple changes might make a world of difference to employee morale, productivity and, inevitably, profits.

1. Give your employees the benefit of doubt

Most corporate environments today are eerily reminiscent of pre-industrial revolution hell holes. Of course, that is an exaggeration, but you get what we mean. The work environment can get extremely stressful, and you do not know why an employee made a mistake he made, until you actually feel it is important to know the cause. Breathe, and communicate. Do not jump to conclusions. Giving your employees the benefit of doubt will also help you give yourself scope for improvement. Maybe you need to do something differently to help your employees perform better. Always be open to that fact.

2. Communication is truly the key

Respond to emails, invest time in meting out detailed feed-back, organize team lunches and dinners, bond. Don't assume that people know your vision, your ideas or plans. Communicate them often. And remember that two monologues don't make a dialogue – communication is a two-way street. Take time to listen, to understand, to discuss. Being a boss can be easy at times, but being a mentor never is. But being a mentor is definitely more valuable for your organization in the longer run, than being a boss.

3. Micromanaging only kills productivity

Not very long ago, we wrote about the importance of delegating tasks, if you have resources and a team at your disposal, learn how to delegate tasks. It will help both you as well as them. Being a control freak always has adverse effects on your productivity levels. It is impossible to micro manage everything. Also, do acknowledge and trust the talent of other people who have been hired because of their skills to handle the particular tasks. By delegating, you achieve two very important things – 1. The **Trust** of your employees 2. **Productivity.**

4. Applaud and motivate your People

The importance of motivating your employees cannot be stressed upon, enough. Letting your employees know that <u>you value them for the great work they do</u>, helps them bring out the best in themselves. You know you are a good leader and a good boss when employees don't want to let you down. It is important to hold slackers accountable, but it is more important to make it a point to applaud your employees frequently, maybe on a weekly basis. Your employees feel valued when you start or end the week by personally communicating one thing you think each member of your team did a good job with. It may not even be something big. Gratitude does go a long way to inspire and motivate.

5. Apologize when you need to

Remember that just because you are the boss, does not mean you are immune from making mistakes. Everyone is prone to mistakes and errors. What is more important is putting your ego of being superior aside, and admitting when things go wrong because of something you did, or could have done differently. Most often managers feel this quality makes them vulnerable. In fact, it is the exact opposite. It empowers you to lead your team in a much more productive manner. Humility scores way over hubris – not only for winning hearts but is also great for the bottom-line.

It can be overwhelming to be the person who is, at the end of the day, going to be held responsible or accountable for the way his/her team performs. This pressure to be a leader not a boss, more often than not gets to you. A little pressure, is of course is healthy. But ask yourself this, would you rather be a boss your employees absolutely loathe and detest? Or be a leader who they feel proud to work for. The world of work can never have enough of those kinds!

About the Author

Jared Sawyer Jr., at the age of 20, acclaims a 15-year career as an entrepreneur, author, and preacher since the age of 5. With millions of YouTube views and 200,000 followers on social media, Jared garners thousands in attendance at his renown youth and young adult conferences annually and has published four books. He has been named by numerous publications as one of the most influential young Christian leaders. You can visit his website at www.jaredsawyerjr.com and find him on Facebook, Twitter, and Instagram.